Yves Bonnefoy

Twayne's World Authors Series
French Literature

David O'Connell, Editor
University of Illinois

Maxwell A. Smith, Editor
University of Chattanooga

TWAS 702

YVES BONNEFOY, 1978
Photograph reproduced by
permission of Yves Bonnefoy

Yves Bonnefoy

By Mary Ann Caws

The Graduate School and University Center
City University of New York

Twayne Publishers • Boston

Yves Bonnefoy

Mary Ann Caws

Copyright © 1984 by G. K. Hall & Company
All Rights Reserved
Published by Twayne Publishers
A Division of G. K. Hall & Company
70 Lincoln Street
Boston, Massachusetts 02111

Book Production by Marne B. Sultz

Book Design by Barbara Anderson

Printed on permanent/durable acid-free
paper and bound in the United States of
America.

Library of Congress Cataloging in Publication Data

Caws, Mary Ann.
  Yves Bonnefoy.

  (Twayne's world authors series; TWAS 702. French
literature)
  Bibliography: p. 109
  Includes index.
  1. Bonnefoy, Yves—Criticism and interpretation.
I. Title.   II. Series: Twayne's world authors series;
TWAS 702.   III. Series: Twayne's world authors series.
French literature.
PQ2603.0533Z6 1984   841'.914   83–22833
ISBN 0–8057–6549–2

for Roy and Ersi Breunig

Contents

About the Author

Distinguished professor of romance languages and comparative literature at Hunter College and at the Graduate Center of the City University of New York, Mary Ann Caws is the executive officer of the doctoral program in French and codirector of the Peyre Institute at the Graduate Center. She has been visiting professor at Princeton University, president of the Association for the Study of Dada and Surrealism, president of the Modern Language Association, and a visiting scholar for Phi Beta Kappa. She is an officer in the Order of the Palmes Académiques, an Honorary Doctor of Humane Letters, is a member of the Board of the American Comparative Literature Association and the visiting committee for romance languages, Harvard University, and is on the advisory council for Princeton University's comparative literature department. She has judged translations for the National Book Award, serves on committees for ACLS, Mellon, and Rockefeller awards, has held fellowships from the Guggenheim Foundation, the Senior Fulbright-Hays program, the American Council of Learned Societies, and the National Endowment for the Humanities, for which she has also directed a Summer Seminar for College Teachers.

Professor Caws is the author of *Surrealism and the Literary Imagination, The Poetry of Dada and Surrealism, André Breton, The Inner Theater of Recent French Poetry, The Surrealist Voice of Robert Desnos, René Char, The Presence of René Char, La Main de Pierre Reverdy, L'Oeuvre filante de René Char, The Eye in the Text: Essays on Perception from Mannerist to Modern, A Metapoetics of the Passage,* and *Reading Frames in Modern Fiction.* She edited and translated *Approximate Man and Other Writings of Tristan Tzara,* and coedited the *Poems of René Char, Roof Slates and Other Poems of Pierre Reverdy, Poems of André Breton, The Prose Poem in France,* and edited *Selected Writings of Stéphane Mallarmé, Poems of Saint-John Perse* and *About French Poetry from Dada to Tel Quel.* She edits the journal *Le Siècle éclaté: études sur dada, le surréalisme et les avant-gardes,* co-edits *Data/Surrealism,* and serves on the advisory board of several other journals, including *Diacritics* and the *French Review.* Her husband, Peter James Caws, is a professor of philosophy.

Introduction: Response

These pages are written not as an act of criticism or of explication, but rather of response. They pay tribute, in a personal fashion however unfashionable, to the highly personal poetry of Yves Bonnefoy and his no less personal and continuing essay on or commentary about and response to art and writing.

"Ripeness is all": so opens Bonnefoy's essay on *King Lear* with a quotation meaningful in that context, and in ours. This volume would be thicker, were it to await Bonnefoy's next critical or poetic works, fuller in the literal sense, but this work needs now no further ripeness.

It is now that we should read him, whether or not we have done so before. I should like the very brevity of this introduction to pay tribute to Bonnefoy's work before us, and even more, with us, in the community of readers of both poetry and art.

The ideas on which Bonnefoy's poetics are based hold in an extremely complex and yet apparently simple equilibrium. Our excarnation outside ourselves, when we are extended in the world by our collective passions, is balanced by our incarnation as we are one with our senses and our intellect; the passion of our art and writing is set against the "unwriting" characteristic of our present critical moment; our literary and artistic past, as it infuses its traditional values into the present by means of intertextual visual and verbal references, may clash with but be included in the future projection of our path. This delicate balance must influence any critical study of Yves Bonnefoy, as that study itself must respond to the various contrary and yet interrelated impulses.

In a writer whose own critical production is known for its perception and deeply human values, the apparent modes of difference—poems and literary essays, tales and critical commentary on art—have their own coherence and even their forms of repetition, so that the reassembling view of what might have seem dispersed efforts retells and recalls an integrity we already sensed, underlying all the parts.

In any commentary on Yves Bonnefoy, a strong emphasis should be laid on the idea of place: the place of the the essay, of the poem,

of the critical vision, and the place of the reader in response to these
texts, each related to a time and a space, a now and a here. Each
image in the world his texts inhabit has the power to key in the
whole, so that one stone, a cloud, or a salamander is able to speak
of far more than itself. So too such commentary should, in fact
must, reach out past its individual parts to the function and the
place of poetry as a whole.

This book concerns Yves Bonnefoy as critic and as poet and as
thinker, but it concerns, more specifically and yet more broadly,
each reading we might bring in turn to these chosen texts. It wills
itself to be far from a static volume, inserting itself deliberately in
the movement it distinguishes within the current of Bonnefoy's
writing and sight. Nor does it make any pretense at objectivity, at
caring equally for all the poems and essays; rather, it deals at length
with the techniques and motifs that appear to this reader to be most
essential ones, believing—and firmly—that in so doing, it best
responds to what this poetry demands of us, and what this critical
thought offers to us, that is, an opportunity to make the best of
ourselves as readers of a deeply moral writing and attitude in and
to a time often gone wrong, without despair or false optimism,
with hope in language as what has formed us and in the image even
as we know its deceptions.

I have tried here to convey the deep significance, moral and
aesthetic, of a writer and thinker and poet of primary importance
to our time, and the time beyond ours.

In some remarkable way, Bonnefoy's criticism, both literary and
artistic, reflects the simple engagement of the poems and the massive
power of a thought fully involved in a morally luminous consid-
eration of what it is to create and to be, here and now on this earth.
As we respond to our actual condition, we transcend it, but never
for some heaven, only for what humans are able to make with human
thought and love and perception. So Bonnefoy suggests we consider
the Tombs of Ravenna for their statement about death as a part of
life and about the lies of the concept, or the abstract idea, that
bloodless refusal of what most counts: being here, using the language
we love, seeing the red cloud Mondrian, for example, taught us to
see, or hearing the ant scurrying across the leaves, as a haiku might
have had us listen to the smallest detail.

As he celebrates the small and the available, as well as what is
unseen but sensed, that back country beyond the one in which we

live, but which—as we feel it present—gives our time and our space its meaning and its loveliness, Bonnefoy makes of himself one of the great teachers as he is already one of the great poets of our time.

Mary Ann Caws

The Graduate School and University Center
City University of New York

Acknowledgments

I am most grateful, above all, to Yves Bonnefoy for his long friendship, and for his willingness to discuss his work and his way of seeing.

My thanks to the Research Foundation of the City University of New York for enabling me to make the voyages and do the thinking, reading, and writing necessary for this project.

All quotations taken, with thanks to the appropriate sources, from the works of Yves Bonnefoy, with Mercure de France, or with the editors mentioned.

When an initial appears after a quotation, the reference is to one of Bonnefoy's books listed in the Bibliography; after the first reference, the page numbers may occur alone in the chapter dealing with the specific work.

Chronology

1923 Yves Bonnefoy born in Tours to Élie and Hélène Bonnefoy. Studies in the local school and in Lycée Descartes in Tours.

1941 Baccalaureate degree in mathematics and philosophy.

1942–1943 Studies higher mathematics and prepares certificate from the Université de Poitiers in general mathematics.

1943 Lives in Paris. Develops interest in poetics. Meets Victor Brauner, Raoul Ubac, and Hans Bellmer, and publishes with a few friends *La Révolution la Nuit,* a surrealist journal. Friendship with Paul Celan, Georges Henein, Gilbert Lély. Reads Georges Bataille, Pierre-Jean Jouve, Dante, the *Book of the Dead,* and the *Popol-Vuh.* Meets André Breton.

1947 Definitive break with surrealism.

1947–1952 Works on his first book of poetry, *Du Mouvement et de l'immobilité de Douve.*

1953 *Douve* appears with the Mercure de France. Marries. Studies philosophy at the Académie de Paris, with Gaston Bachelard for the philosophy of science, Jean Wahl, and Jean Hyppolite for Hegel and Gilson. Thesis on Baudelaire and Kierkegaard. Continues studies of mathematics. New interest in art. Travels in Italy and works on Piero, Palladio, Caravaggio, the baroque artists, and Poussin.

1954 *Peintures murales de la France gothique.*

1957–1968 Translates Shakespeare.

1958 *Hier régnant désert.*

1959 *L'Improbable.*

1961 Essay on *Arthur Rimbaud.* Meets Pierre-Jean Jouve, André du Bouchet, Philippe Jaccottet, and Jacques Dupin. Edits *L'Éphémère* with du Bouchet and Dupin (in 1960s).

1965   *Pierre écrite.* Remarries. Discovers the region of the
       Basses-Alpes, of great significance for him and for his
       subsequent writing.

1966   Writes *Rome, 1930* (published in 1970).

1967   *Un rêve fait à Mantoue.*

1972   *L'Arrièrè-Pays.*

1975   *Dans le leurre du seuil.*

1977   *Le Nuage rouge. Rue traversière.* Teaches, in these years,
       in Geneva, Vincennes, Nice, and Aix-en-Provence,
       and at Yale.

1981   Appointed to Chair of Comparative Studies of the
       Poetic Function, Collège de France. *Entretiens sur la
       poésie.*

Biographical Note

Yves Bonnefoy was born on 24 June 1923 in Tours. His father, Élie, worked in the locomotive factory there. His mother, Hélène, whose maiden name was Maury, was a substitute teacher for a number of years, but when she was widowed in 1936, she was given a full-time position in a village of the Cher valley, about fifteen miles from Tours. Both parents were of peasant origin from the Quercy region of Rouergue; Yves's maternal grandfather, the son of a shepherdess, had become a teacher in the village, when this was considered a sign of progress, under the reign of Kantian rationality.

Bonnefoy's parents had come to work in a place not quite so impoverished, and had a daughter, older than Yves by several years, who encouraged her brother to read the authors in her school assignments and in inexpensive editions. They lived in a little street near the railway tracks which was destroyed during the last war. This childhood, described in *L'Arrière-Pays* (The country beyond), was shared between this new home and their original one, returned to on vacations, and which seemed the true one. His grandfather, now retired, lived with the remains of his little scholarly museum and his few books, some of which he had written for his pleasure, and copied and bound himself (he also made his own furniture), in a vast house near the River Lot, among the plumtrees and the vines. All this was important to his grandson's imagination and his growing knowledge about the world.

Bonnefoy carried on his studies at the nearby school, then at the Lycée Descartes in Tours, where he was a day boarder, between the morning and evening trains. After his baccalauréat, in math and philosophy in 1941, he studied advanced mathematics, and worked also at the Université de Poitiers on a certificate in general math. He did not intend to enter the École normale or the École Polytechnique, for which he did not prepare the exams (he detested chemistry) but simply to acquire a knowledge in mathematics, which he liked. At the end of 1943 he went to Paris, intending to continue his degree work, but was diverted from that by his increased poetic interests.

Bonnefoy began to write, particularly poems, in early childhood, and in 1941, the reading of some surrealist works, especially those of Paul Éluard, which seemed to serve as a "key to the poetry of his century." On his arrival in Paris, he found some painters of the surrealist group which had already dispersed—Victor Brauner, Raoul Ubac, Hans Bellmer a little later—and published with two or three young friends a little review called *La Révolution la Nuit (Revolution at Night)*, which remained within the orthodox lineage of the movement.

He formed some lasting friendships that were important for his development, including that with Christian Dotremont, who published in Brussels and then in Paris, his own journal on the fringes of surrealism, *Les Deux Soeurs (The Two Sisters)*, where Bonnefoy published an *Éclairage objectif (Objective Lighting);* with Georges Henein, who came back every year from Cairo, where he published *La Part du sable (The Sand's Part);* with Paul Celan, and with Gilbert Lély, rigorous and encouraging. This was also the time of some essential readings, among them, Georges Bataille, Pierre-Jean Jouve, Dante, some archaic texts (the *Popol Voh,* in Raynaud's translation, which moved him greatly; the Egyptian *Book of the Dead;* the *Kalevala,* which Jousse quoted in his lessons of the anthropology of the gesture), and above all Chestov, whose *Power of the Keys* contributed greatly to detaching Bonnefoy from surrealism. Encouraged by Brauner, Bonnefoy met André Breton soon after the latter returned from New York, but for some reason this relationship did not flourish; Bonnefoy did not enjoy the meetings of the surrealist group, and he left surrealism in 1947, on the eve of the International Exhibition, after refusing to sign the manifesto *Rupture inauragurale (Inaugural Rupture)* on that occasion.

In 1947–52 Bonnefoy worked on his first book of poetry, *Du mouvement et de l'immobilité de Douve (Of the Motion and the Immobility of Douve)*, closely related to some prose writings in the form of tales, "L'Agent secret," "Le Voyageur," "L'Ordalie," and others; these were finally absorbed, at least for a time, in his poetic writings. Adrienne Monnier, whose bookstore Bonnefoy frequented, solicited from him a book for the collection which she headed at the Mercure de France, and *Douve* was published in 1953 under the Mercure imprint. (The Mercure still publishes his books.)

When he was first married, Bonnefoy worked at the Academy of Paris, and was led to study philosophy, notably with Gaston Bachelard for the philosophy of science, Jean Wahl, and Hyppolite on Hegel, as well as Serrus and the works of Gilson. His degree, the diploma of which he subsequently destroyed, was on Baudelaire and Kierkegaard. During this time his studies in mathematics continued at the library, got off track, and finally ended, not without his regretting it deeply. After Bonnefoy's first trips to Italy, he acquired new interests, first the study of perspectives in the fourteenth and fifteenth centuries, particularly of Piero della Francesca, then the study of Michelangelo, Palladio, Caravaggio, the baroque artists, Poussin, all in relation to Byzantium and Romanesque art, a relation somewhat obscure but which seemed essential to him. He sensed above all how closely the image is related to the poetic word.

After the publication of his first book at the Mercure de France, Bonnefoy met Pierre-Jean Jouve, who was just entering that publishing house. He also met André du Bouchet, whom he had only glimpsed in the preceding years, and a little later met Philippe Jaccottet and Jacques Dupin. In the circle of these poetic affections and a few others—Boris de Schloezer, Louis René des Forêts, Gaetan Picon, Jean Starobinski—most of the enterprises with which Bonnefoy has associated himself in the last few years have been inscribed, in particular, the publication of the journal *L'Éphémère* in the 1960s.

In these years Bonnefoy undertook, among other projects, a study of the Gothic murals in France, and then a series of translations of Shakespeare. Poetically, he went from *Hier régnant désert* (Yesterday the Desert Reigning) of 1958 to *Pierre écrite (Written Stone)* in 1965, and from the essays of the *Improbable* in 1959, completed by *Rimbaud,* in 1961, to those of *Un rêve fait à Mantoue* (A dream in Mantua) in 1967. After he remarried and was writing *Pierre écrite* and *Un rêve fait à Mantoue,* he discovered some regions in the Basses-Alpes to which he felt immediately attached, and where he lived for long periods. *Dans le leurre du seuil* (In the threshold's lure) of 1975, where the experience of these ten years is summed up, is full of it, but *L'Arrière-Pays* (The country beyond) of 1972, and even *Rome 1630,* written in 1966, bear its mark.

Subsequently Bonnefoy published *Le Nuage rouge* (The red cloud), a series of essays, *La Rue Traversière* (Short-cut street), a collection of tales and prose poems, and a study on the plastic arts responding to the essays of Georges Duthuit, whose work he has recently reedited and whose early writings he prefaced. Bonnefoy has recently edited a large encyclopedia of mythology for Flammarion, as well as written

essays for art books on Bellini and Mantegna, and for an anthology
of Haiku. Published in 1981, his *Entretiens sur la poésie* (Interviews
about poetry) provides a good idea of his continuing thought on
poetic forms, ideas, and problems.

In recent years, Bonnefoy has held visiting professorships in Geneva, Vincennes, Nice, and Aix-en-Provence; in America, he held
short-term professorships at Brandeis, Wesleyan, and Yale. He is
now a professor at the Collége de France in Paris, where he occupies
the Chair of Comparative Studies of the Poetic Function.

The information for this Biographical Note was adapted from
Bonnefoy's resumé of his life in the collection *Poetes d'Aujourd'hui*
(Seghers), at the suggestion of the poet.

Chapter One

Continuities:
The Place and the Path

> . . . the path, from then on, toward this
> invisible forward, which is the place.
>
> (*NR*, 76)

Like the spiral form, one of the characteristics of baroque architecture—to which form he refers with enthusiasm—Bonnefoy's own way of thinking and writing seems to expand over an ever greater surface, while starting with similar points of reference. "Recouvrir sa vie": to recover and to regain one's own life, and with it the diverse modes of being and expression—this might well be the goal of a writer only self-concerned. Bonnefoy's own impulses toward the essay, story, the dream tale, and the poem, are coherently gathered in a "changing relation to objects and beings, through the development of an experience of language," as Jean Starobinski phrases it in his introduction to Bonnefoy's poetic anthology for Gallimard. Thus the accumulating imagery and vocabulary of path and of voyage, and all that we associate with the idea of quest: setting off and returning, the *topoi* of the great myths, but also all the myriad entrances, the doors, the gardens, and the deserts.

But the great myths are made of the simplest things and terms. Such simple words as he uses—those of bread and wine, of house and storm and stone—enter into communion with each other, as Bonnefoy says, and are able to transcend the rigid network of the concept, fixed and frozen, dead or dying. From these few and strong words, in their very simplicity, "of these assumptions and these symbols, a place will be made that, although it is nothing in its final substance, serves nonetheless as our completed form, marking therefore a unity in act and in being's own absolute to come. Incarnation, exterior to the dream, is near at hand" (*NR*, 278–79).

Such essential words, and others, constitute a great danger, in spite of their apparent possibility of a secular salvation: "If we devote ourselves to the words telling of hearth, tree, path, or wandering and return, that will not necessarily deliver us; even in a sacralized world, the spirit of possession can be born once more, making presence once again an object, making of a living knowledge a science once more, and therefore impoverished. . ." (*NR, 342*). But we will build, through poetry, a world from and for those words, in their simplicity and their concrete reality.

Words are to be treated like images, to which a few general caveats apply. Images share the danger of apparent possession and of rigidity: they must, therefore, be kept not just simple but fluid and open, exchanging their symbolic values as their real ones, always keeping their exceptional power of interpenetration. They are not to be reduced to any one meaning or kept in any one place.

The fluidity of words and of images makes, in a paradoxical sense, their strength and their carrying power. So the ideas on which Bonnefoy's poetics is based are themselves balanced, opposed, and interchangeable. The *excarnation* he speaks of, as we are outside ourselves and extended in the world and in our collective passions and justice, is balanced by an *incarnation,* our being one with our senses, our intellect with our bodies. The past infusing its traditional values into the present, by means of epigraphs and intertextual references, is balanced by future projection. Even the art and the passion of writing are to be balanced by those of unwriting (*écrire* set off against *désécrire*). In each case, the continuity from one way or mode of being and expression to the next is itself balanced by and exemplified in the continuity between these same oppositional terms.

As one term and one mode relate to the next, so all are reassembled after they seem to diverge; the mode of quest is also one of return, and the mode of difference one of repetition. Bonnefoy's whole corpus in all its various manifestations could be inscribed under the terms of recall and repetition, of reassembling and retelling, of relation and return.

Finally—as an introduction to the following chapters arranged, roughly, by genre—the genre categories overlap and yet are always different. Each experience is extended through its various ways of being perceived; however, the place and substance of the poem are shared with that of the essay and the tale and the dream. At the conclusion of these chapters, the true place of sojourn will still lie, not just before us, but ahead.

Chapter Two
The Poet and the Voice
From Movement to Yesterday

L'Anti-Platon (The Anti-Plato), an odd series of nine brief prose poems published in 1947, opens with a call to human specificity, in opposition to the realm of vague Platonic Ideas. Bonnefoy will never relax his concern with the particular, and even in moments of his greatest temptation toward another land, a crossroads to another life, he maintains his visible loyalty to the here and now, to this land and the range of things which are its furnishings, seen in detail or in a wider perspective.

"And now this object: a horse's head larger than life, containing a whole town, with its streets and its ramparts running along between the eyes, wedding the winding path to the length of the nose" (*AP*, 11). Like a contemporary *vanitas,* the object here is a stark reminder of mortality or *memento mori,* including a death skull, a candle, and a glass; a meaningful and typical assortment of symbols of everyday living and its necessary end, this vision is all the more terrible in that a horse's head replaces the ordinary human skull, as if in mockery. Moreover, the everydayness is intensified; the tiny model town is more "civilized" and organized than the usual assortment of miscellaneous things which would be placed upon the vanity table by the skull, while its insertion into the animal head sets up an anamorphic play between two ways of seeing, between the animal and the cultural. As for the balance between and real and the artificial, the town is constructed of wood and cardboard, but illuminated, on the bias (still the unsettling angle of "this thing"), by the real moon. Then suddenly the anamorphic play is accentuated by the skull's turning into a woman's head, turning on the disc of a phonograph. Multiple forms of intensification are used here: surprise, aggrandization (of the head by the town inside it), substitution (of the animal for the human), and then resubstitution (of the human construction for the animal). When a woman's head replaces the horse's head, more horrible still in its chaotic appearance with the hair streaming about the wildly turning head upon the phonograph, the music of harmony is replaced by this melodramatic disharmony.

The presentation is deliberately shocking in its offsets and contrasts: this initial image is followed by the peace of the reeds, the stone, and the water of the countryside, the calm suddenly interrupted by the last images: "robes tachées" ("spotted dresses"), blood-covered laughter, and the absence of any gaze whatsoever. Such a horrible absence and equally horrible presence provide an unequaled combination of "choses d'ici," or earthly things, weighing in the long run more than the perfection of Ideas. The anti-Platonic theme initiates a violence full of uneasy and monstrous forms: a hatchet falls, the woman'a head is thrown into flames, and a statue of blood is sacrificed by knife edge to a "funereal dialectic" or rebirth and division (13). The country, once seen with its water and stones, is now composed of blood, blackened flesh and death: death as the illuminating wound, which, by the certainty of suffering, clarifies all about it, including the subjective and occasionally ambivalent world of poetry. Here it provides also a theater for the struggle of love and death, a dramatic *liebestod* to be taken up again in a broader sweep, within the nineteen parts of the *Mouvement et immobilité de Douve,* for which this earlier poem is in some sense a preparation—a few images recur: the penetration of the body into summer, the black grass "like a funereal cloak," a cry, the fissure in the earth. Illumination also, because, surrounded by a set of teeth buried in the earth, this stone at the middle of it all, this touchstone of sacrifice, lies at the very center of the turning world: "From having touched this stone the lamps of the world spin, the secret lighting circulates" (19).

The theater of the death of Douve, the name signifying at once a depression in the ground and woman's proper name, is sketched in the opening section of *Du Mouvement et de l'Immobilité de Douve (Of the Movement and the Immobility of Douve,* 1953), which enlarges upon the nine sections of the poem just mentioned. Douve is surely one of the most haunting of contemporary literary creations, for she takes shape all at once in an unforgettable scene of violence and pathos and love. She is seen running, battling the wind, and being torn apart by the forces of death. It is once again summer, and the sun and wind spotlight specific gestures, as the ivy, this simple image torn and bruised, appearing in the essays as the very signal of presence itself, is chosen over any vague Idea: ("rather the ivy"). We remember from the preceding volume that Platonic Ideas cannot approach the strength of the specific object, either for violence or for affection, and can "only tinge the lips." It is only in the small details—a sunny patch left on a windowpane at the coming of night, a spot of light upon a mountain, or a single leaf of an unnamed tree or its accompanying ivy—that life is felt as something beyond a generality, and as the transcendence, already, of the death to come. And yet the specificity is accompanied by the very incompletion of such statements as "Rather the ivy. . . . Rather the wind. . . . Rather, on some mountainside. . . ." They are left open to all possible comparisons. Rather than what?—the choice may be made elsewhere, but it need not be specified here, and the preference seems all the stronger for the incompletion.

The poem is anything but gentle: the wind is stronger than any memory, so that the present occupies the entire scene. The dress blows about, in tongues of flames, until the beating wings of wind and their exultation are perceived as celebrating both death and life. But directly after this violent "beating" wind, the poet describes the rain beating down, as the heart beat before. Wind and rain, dream and vision mix in a natural metaphor and a human reaction. Douve's gestures, immemorial and luminous, those of deathless beauty and ceaseless birth, then slow down: "Gestures of Douve, already slower, black gestures" (27). In seeking death, she somehow clarifies life. For the opposites will always meet within Bonnefoy's vision, especially in this period: with rain and a subterranean river there mixes the "fire" of her gestures; this arm inflames, is raised, and falls; the shadow and the mist cover over the gaze shared by the woman and the poet.

Now the pounding of the arteries, within which are felt the beating down of rain and the roll of drums, is replaced by a terrible and disintegrating music in her hands, knees, head, as the facial muscles dislocate, the eyes are ripped out, and the body is extended horribly under a swarm of insects. Even the dress, once pure and flaming, is now soiled from the oil of the lamp: the morbidity of the imagery prepares the rôle of the poet as watcher, as the observer of her secret knowledge—of the ceaseless corruption of her eyes, now clouding over. The strident "exultation" of insects is now heard in an atrocious music, displacing all images to leave behind only an imageless truth, as the insects advance in an endless pitiless assault upon the body. Resplendent with a somber fire, she has access to regions lower and lower as the violence and the horror subside.

Solemnly and not without grandeur, an incantation in the form of a hymn to death now rises, marked by anaphoric final repetition: *now, now, now,* drawing attention to the vividness of the moment, this "présence exacte":

Le ravin pénètre dans la bouche maintenant,
Les cinq doigts se dispersent en hasards de forêts maintenant,
La tête première coule entre les herbes maintenant
. . . et c'est nous dans ce vent dans cette eau dans ce froid maintenant.
(39)

(The ravine penetrates the mouth now,
The five fingers are dispersed in forest random now,
The head first of all slips among the grass now,
. . . and we are in this wind in this water in this cold now.)

The observer and the reader are drawn into the salutation of earth, which appears to have neither sadness nor resignation to it. The blood, appearing exactly where the poem is said to tear apart, renders the poem living, and in the intensely oxymoronic atmosphere already pointed out—flame/cold, birth/death— tension marks the fitting site for trial. As if the poem were some matter to be rent asunder, on which to inflict damage and thus prove the vitality of the stuff inside: "You had to appear at the secret border of a funereal place where your light dims; you had to submit to trial" (40). Along with the dying figure in the poem, the poem undergoes the trial of death, in order to live. Even the death "infused in her laughter" only contributes to the dazzle and brilliance of her theatrical gestures: she, and the poem, pass the test.

Finally, this Douve is seen as an aperture, cut into the world, and into its thickness, an opening through which we learn to perceive. She is the first figure loved and lost as the drama opens, always, through her presence even at her most faraway instants, denying absence and unfeeling in the world about her, forcing awareness upon an erstwhile numbness: thus her description as an "ouverture dans l'épaisseur du monde" ("opening in the thickness of the world"). Nevertheless, the tragedy of this poem is essential:

a nineteenth part, coming directly after the concluding encounter of poet and the dazzling vision, and written in two stanzas of free verse instead of the prose of the preceding eighteen parts, contains the history of an attempt at our own evasion of the everyday into another zone: breathing the initial cold, perceiving afresh, we rise into another atmosphere, but are only momentarily able to imitate a figure's flight, falling back again upon the ground like a wounded bird or an arrow whose feathers break at a touch, like some lesser Icarus or some Phoenix in utter failure.

The passing of the world's opacity into perception was, after all, only attempted through the gesture of another, and we cannot possibly imitate or reincarnate another's triumphant bareness; if, then, the final test of perception is to be identification with the flight and fate of another figure, no matter how close, we are to fail. Imagination, admiration, even union, are not the genuine mutual interpenetration of that denseness of the phenomenal world which we most passionately desired. Myths are not so easily transformed into realization: the essential solitude of this poem gives to the title its fullest poignancy: in a theater, one observes, identifies in imagination, but remains an observer. Poetic perception is not necessarily, at least not so far, action.

Of course, the volume does not end there, neither with the theater nor in the observer's failure as actor. The voice of the poet will from now on address itself to other things than to the failure of identification: the gestures of dying, once so dazzling to the onlooker, are now echoed in a section of "Derniers gestes" ("Last Gestures"). The travel of Douve beyond death on a path of trees, these closing after her in order to guarantee her continued brightness even as she becomes nothing, across the river Lethe of forgetfulness along the path she only can take, "this going / Along so much night and in spite of all this river" (43), links her fate to that of the narrator, through the mediation of nature and the word.

For these gestures of crossing and those made by the poet, like some ancient rite of passage, and the gestures of linking already signaled by the image of the threshold, which will be all-important in Bonnefoy's work and to which the last chapter of this book refers, are like the *gesta* of the medieval *chanson de geste:* deeds recounted, lending dignity to the telling word and guaranteeing both to teller and listener emotional participation. The brief verses following the grave salute to the parting gesture of Douve are eloquent:

> Que saisir sinon qui s'échappe,
> Que voir sinon qui s'obscurcit,
> Que désirer sinon qui meurt,
> Sinon qui parle et se déchire? (44)

> (What to seize but what is escaping,
> What to see but what is darkening
> What to desire but what is dying
> Speaking and tearing itself apart?)

Silence is above all the object of desire, the word heard and seen as departing always. What is not repeated and not glimpsed again beyond its own temporary moment is infused with nostalgia and longing, as in Baudelaire's sonnet to the passerby, to which Bonnefoy so often refers: "Ô toi que j'eusse aimée / Ô toi qui le savais!" ("You whom I would have loved / You who knew it!")

The single possible offering acceptable to the person departing forever, as to the dead, would be a speech cast in its very materiality like a blanket "over origin and night." A Maenad consumed by fire in her dancing, Douve disappears by her name into her action to which the poet is the only witness, as she hurls herself into the flames of the sea. This clash of elements is responsible for her intense verticality lit from above, as if we were seeing the dance from some terrace or parapet far above the water where she is hurled. So contemplated, she is at once fleeting, as in a game, and in an attitude of supplication, as in the ancient representations of Maenads. The somber light and the flickering fire place her desolation in a still theatrical setting: "Tout se défait, pensai-je, tout s'éloigne" ("Everything is undone, I thought, everything takes its distance," 50).

And then it is a question of nomination: "Vrai nom" ("True Name"). The True Name given to the dead reminds us of the true place spoken of elsewhere, and leads to the "Vrai Corps" ("True Body"): the act of naming is the essential act of this poetry, and only the poet can effectively name. As a double act of love and hostility, of spirituality and materiality, of freeing and of tying down, the poet opposes her even as he names her: "I am your enemy who will show no pity" (51). Through interdependence of contraries, even the purest words depend upon matter, as spirit depends upon body, meaning upon naming, poetry upon presence and upon the acknowledgment of death inserted in life: "Il te faudra franchir la

mort pour que tu vives, / La plus pure présence est un sang répandu"
("In order to live you must traverse death, / The purest presence is
a blood spilled forth," 52). The full sense of the epigraph from
Hegel at the outset of the volume is understood at present: "But
the life of the spirit is not frightened before death and does not
keep itself pure of it. It is bearing death and maintaining itself
within it" (21). In the privileged or true place of poetry for the
accomplishment of the sacrificial ritual, the true act, preparatory to
the successful flight of the Phoenix, is joyous, all-powerful and self-
perpetuating as the Phoenix is self-resurrecting. With the bird, the
poet's song endures, and the voices echo, one against the other: that
of Douve, of the bird, of death and life. The meditation on naming
implies in the same speaking voice the poet, the listener, and the
respondent. Each is called upon to recognize this death or "lowest
marriage," which buries the bright destiny in the earth, Douve in
death, and the poet in her knowledge and in her name: "Douve, je
parle en toi; et je t'enserre / Dans l'acte de connaître et de nommer"
("Douve, I speak in you; and I hold you close / In the act of knowing
and of naming," 55). Douve answers, in self-containment, within
her own silence and lack of sight: "Pourtant ce cri sur moi vient de
moi, / Je suis muré dans mon extravagance" ("Yet this cry upon
me comes from my own self, / I am walled in my own extravagance,"
57).

But against the charged dialogue of poet and victim—whether
a victim of destiny or of self or of the act of poetry itself—other
voices are raised. Unspecified except as "a voice, another voice,"
they serve at once as parts of a tragic chorus, representing outside
and in, exteriorising Douve's point of view upon herself, the poet's
other aspects, and, perhaps above all, a questioning of the gestural
and verbal *signs* uttered so far. "Long have I retreated before you,
signs," says one voice, and another: "What sign are you bringing
on your black lips?" I shall inhabit you, it continues, lifting you
to yet another emptiness. But these are not negative cries of death
and distress, rather, "distant beneficent voices" of dawn and rain,
waking the clay figures along the longing earth, expressing fruit-
fulness even in the act of dying.

Douve, waking from her hypnotic state as stone, having shared
its blindness, now sees her own drama clarified in the dying and
suffering which is the sure way to the mind. Reassured by day, by
the summer and the naked earth, she calls upon silence once more

after these voices are heard, forged as they are in the hearth of
contraries. Her invocation to cold and death is ardent in its tone,
made with "reddening words":

> Que le verbe s'éteigne
> Dans cette pièce basse où tu me rejoins,
> Que l'âtre du cri se resserre
> Sur nos mots rougeoyants.

> Que le froid par ma mort se lève et prenne un sens. (63)

> (Let the word die out
> In this low room where you join me,
> Let the hearth of the cry narrow in
> Upon our reddening words.

> Let cold through my death rise up and take on meaning.)

The imploration gathers up all the strength of the preceding voices,
and is answered by a further sign of the interdependence of perception and of speech (64). The watcher keeps vigil in the speaker, as
death in life and life in death. He implores for Douve the destruction
she has already invoiced, echoing her speech act: "Demande pour
tes yeux que les rompe la nuit" ("Ask, for your eyes, that night
shall break them," 66). But the verbal command is followed by a
doubt as to the efficacy of the word, expressed by one of the voices:
"Oui, c'est bientôt périr de n'être que parole, / Et c'est tâche fatale
et vain couronnement" ("Yes, being but word means to perish
soon, / And is a fatal task and vain coronation").

And yet this doubt is itself balanced by one of the most celebrated
images recurring in Bonnefoy's work, that of the orangerie, that
"site far off" where the salamander acts as Phoenix, assuring presence
and resurrection, living through the fire. It is appropriate that after
the ways of death and their insertion into life, the place of poetry
should appear again. The orangerie is allied, as both contrary and
complement, to the Ordalie or medieval trial. This ritual and the
orangerie itself allow easy access: the latter is marked by a vase on
its threshold, placed in welcome to the wanderer as to the reader,
for whom, also, "words of healing" will be recited: "Let a place be
made for the one approaching, / A person cold and deprived of a
dwelling" (85). The place is a true place, "un vrai lieu," but also

a place of combat: in its perfect form, the orangerie invites a meditation of the mythical. The salamander desired by Douve is celebrated in a luminously erotic series of prose statements. She desires
penetration by the narrow animal, desires both blindness and possession; but at the same time she is herself the salamander, immobile
and knowing. The single vigil kept over the dead and through the
dying ("I keep watch in you") leads to a double vigil at the summit
of the winter's night. The wound (of knowledge, of love, and of
their penetration by each other) marks the moment of sacrifice, and
the woman as well as the hollow which she also signifies, receive
once more their identical name: "Et maintenant tu es Douve" ("And
now you are Douve," 74); "Douve sera ton nom" ("Douve will be
your name," 82). "Justice" and "Truth" precede a poem called "True
Place", and in that truest place of the orangerie now named, Douve
will be laid.

So the true place "where everything is unveiled" or disclosed (as
in the Heideggerian sense of being made apparent or "called into
disclosedness") contains war and repose, specificity and abstraction.
The orangerie can be represented anywhere, and it then becomes
the true place; for instance, the Chapel Brancacci suggests the
powerful image of "vigil-lamp of January," casting its light upon
the tiled floor, as the shadow all about and the dark frescoes provide
a place suited to the search for eternity within what can be grasped
here and now, in one of the privileged sites for the imagination:
"Ce que je tiens serré n'est peut-être qu'une ombre, / Mais sache y
distinguer un visage éternel" ("What I hold tight is perhaps only
a shadow, / But discern in it an eternal face," 86). The play of light
and shadow here leads to the final poems of "lieu" or place concluding the volume: "Lieu du combat" ("Place of Combat"), where
the knight of sorrow becomes the brother "whose face is sought
near all fountains," whose death is equivalent to nocturnal shadow,
and against whose suffering the truth of dawn and day must be
measured. And this is now the "Lieu de la Salamandre" ("Place of
the Salamander"), whose awareness traverses fire and with whose
purity and silence the poet is intimate, calling it his accomplice
and his own thought, wedded to the flame in an allegory of risk
and joy beyond wordlessness itself.

Finally, the "Vrai lieu du cerf" ("True Place of the Deer") is
charged with the weight of religious myth, recalling the medieval
allegory of Christ as the deer pursued by hunters, and escaping. All

that is implied in this ending of a volume on death and what traverses it in a deeply poetic consciousness: "Ô notre force et notre gloire, pourrez-vous / Trouer la muraille des morts?" ("Oh our strength and our glory, shall you / Pierce the wall of the dead?" 91).

Much of the strength and carrying power of Bonnefoy's work lies in its intense emphasis on polar opposites: for example, the movement and immobility in Douve's title, or the rest and combat visible in the poems, or the purity and the eroticism of the salamander, which are then absorbed each into the other. The poetic process is similar to the one by which the poet has his vision *through* Douve or speaks within her, or even lives in her ("I shall find out how to dwell in you," 59); and yet the ambiguities remain. For instance, from Douve: "If this night is other than the night" (60), implying a tension between specificity and generality, and nevertheless also the common ground between them, that undeniably links night to night, beyond any specificity or distinction.

The ambiguous relation of the other and the same is stressed by Douve's question as to what voice is speaking near her or against her, naming her, and by her subsequent claim about being the origin of all she hears; "Yet this cry upon me comes from myself." Furthermore, the words said by one of the unidentified voices could be said of this poem as a whole, and its coherence as an inseparable unit, for the voices are, all of them, part of the rhapsody. The volume, rewritten with several linking passages for its final form in 1978 after its initial publication in 1953, makes now a complete narration whose harmonies are complex, moving, and ardent: "I have borne my word within you as a flame" (67). The very speaking and narrating of the Death and poetry of Douve into the arduous shadows, like consciousness into dark, compose this elegy, like the name Virginia Woolf was tempted to give to her novels, which sets ablaze by its spirit the silence before and after.

Readers tend to be greatly divided as to their opinions of the successive volumes of Bonnefoy's poetry, some preferring *Douve* for its incantatory power and dramatic sequence, some preferring the condensed inscriptions of *Pierre écrite (Written Stone)*, some the continuities and imagery of the massive *Dans le Leurre du seuil* (In the lure of the threshold), Bonnefoy's most recent long poetic work at the time of this writing. The brief volume about to be discussed, *Hier Régnant Désert* (Yesterday the desert reigning, 1958), might, on the other hand, appeal to the reader who would choose brevity, depth of feeling, and an indescribable tone of melancholy conveyed by an essential understatement. The poem of yesterday never leads to a statement entire, but only to the threshold of a place where it might have been made.

The title of the initial poem here, called "Menaces du témoin," places the reader immediately at risk, for the observation itself leaves no place for uninvolvement. The fear and blindness within the poem as stated come to paralyze the watcher also, even the one who would by choice remain upon the sidelines. In this text, destruction is paired with the cessation of combat, age with immobility and lone-liness, made parallel to the retraction of mental and physical warmth by the image of the fire receding. The withdrawal of the flame, but also of such strength as the emotion of fright might itself bring, enables the growth of the person, and implicitly, the deepening of the poem equated with the interior experience of language at its most profound. But the static menace hangs heavy in the cessation of all things, in the decrescendo of the dying down in word and wind: "Puis j'ai vieilli. Dehors, vérité de parole / Et vérité de vent ont cessé leur combat" ("Then have I aged. Outside, truth of word / And truth of wind have ceased their battle," 95).

After the first-person lamentation, the narrator addresses a second bystander implied in the battle with questions as to motivation and identity and place: ("Où es-tu, qui es-tu?") associated with the garden of memory and the shadow included in the shadow, pre-sumably within the watching self. The notion enframed in the poem comes to a halt abruptly, as the poem is haunted by its own closure, encapsulated in the repetition of "même . . . même":

> Vois, déjà tous chemins que tu suivais se ferment,
> Il ne t'es plus donné même ce répit
> D'aller même perdu. Terre qui se dérobe
> Est le bruit de tes pas qui ne progressent plus.
>
> . . . .
>
> Tu cesses de venir dans ce jardin,
> Les chemins de souffrir et d'être seul s'effacent. . . . (96–97)

(See, already all the paths you took are closing,
You are no longer given even this respite

Of going even lost. Earth which slips away
Is the sound of your steps which go on no longer.

. . . .

You stop coming in this garden,
The paths of suffering and of loneliness fade out. . . .)

The gradual slowing down, the closing off of possibilities, the blind-
ing of paths and former illuminations and revelations: "Il te suffit /
De mourir longuement comme en sommeil" ("It is enough / For
you to die slowly as in sleep," 97), all these elements which could,
from any traditional perspective, be seen as negative, are here trans-
muted by the tone itself, noble, resigned, but remarkably strong
in the telling and narrating voice. Quite unlike the tone of the
words addressed to Douve in her pilgrimage to a land beyond death
and her laying-to-rest in the orangerie, the elegy—if it can be called
that—to and of a lost being here includes an interrogation new in
this poetry: "Es-tu celui qui meurt, toi qui n'as plus d'angoisse, /
Es-tu même perdu, toi qui ne cherches pas?" ("Are you the one who
dies, anguished no more, / Are you even lost, who do not seek?"
98).

The loss is far from certain, and there are no dramatic gestures,
no disintegration such as is evident in *Douve:* only question and
quiet, as the wind falls still and the fire of the word is laid. This
is the continuation of Kierkegaard's "Knight of Sorrow," whose
premonition we heard already in *Douve.* The rod or the arm is and
will remain the surest weapon for vanquishing in both the fields of
erotic love and combat, and for the construction of a timeless,
spaceless, limitless warmth and radiance, in the dwelling of poetry.

In the next poems, the solitude remains, together with the silence;
yet the oath of construction, recently sworn, is not undone. The
knight renounces glory, fame, distinction, to choose obscurity and
another kind of song, as yet unheard. The grey waters on the shifting
earth match his renunciation, paralleled by the demythification of
the Phoenix, who himself tires of being the self-resurrecting bird
and gives in to his age-old wound, thus undoing himself and his
legend as well as his lie, accepting in their place silence, age, and
death: "L'oiseau se défera par misère profonde . . . / Il vieillira
. . . / Il se taira . . . / Il saura bien mourir . . ." ("The bird will

undo himself in deepest misery . . . / He will grow old . . . / He
will fall silent . . . / He will know how to die. . . ," 102).

But renunciation by the bird of his myth, by the knight of his
renown, do not rule out remorse: rather they increase it. The light
of summer in its mingled sweetness and fear has left its radiant
mark upon the poem and upon all it surrounds and contains: regret,
remorse, and the deepest longing for what is no more. The summer
is wounded in the greyest of its dawns, and the poetry, grave:

> Ce fut un bel été, fade, brisant et sombre,
> Tu aimas la douceur de la pluie en été.
> . . . .
> Et ton orgueil aima cette lumière neuve,
> L'ivresse d'avoir peur sur la terre d'été. (105)

> (The summer was lovely, pale, somber in its shattering,
> You loved the softness of the summer rain.
> . . . .
> And your spirit loved this novel light,
> The excitement of fearing upon the summer earth.)

In the final invocation, a poverty contrary to all the former pride
in poetry and in things previously loved brings about a difference.
As bareness breaks and remakes the spirit, this voluntary renunciation in flames within the desert tables of writing, sets them afire
with an inalienable loneliness: alone, the knight finds no appease-
ment (107).

The title "Le visage mortel" ("The Mortal Face") designates death
already inscribed upon the visage of being; by the poem, the flame
is returned to the somber daylight, as if its ardor were to be undone
by the light of day. Beauty is here dishonored and dispossessed as
it ruins being and undoes the joy of the daily. All things are changed
and oddly opposed in preparation for the Ordalie, that medieval
trial (already compared to the *other* of the orangerie) where the voice
falls into contradiction with itself, and then into the silence seen
as the ultimate grandeur; so is belief to be tested. The sword is
pulled from the stone, in a simple statement of a renewed Arthurian
gesture. In the poetic universe where the interchanges of word and
self are heightened, the essential "grayness of the word" is to be
penetrated only by the ardent "red iron of being" for hospitality
and communion: "Nous venions de toujours . . ." ("We were com-

ing from always . . . ," 103); "Et j'ai rompu ce pain où l'eau lointaine coule" ("And I broke this bread where the distant water runs," 116). The other surrounding gestures are simple, solitary, and therefore honored: praying, keeping the fire, standing guard, or waiting, gestures of the beseeching *orante,* the weeping *pleureuse,* the faithful *veilleur* watching, the dutiful *servante,* the mysterious Parque who controls our fate. The very simplicity of the tasks is moving: watching the fire and sweeping the hearth are the duties of a vestal virgin; just so, the protective gestures of the figure of large stature who comes to participate "in the stone," holding the lamp and leaning over. Gray stones and cold trees surround these acts in which the observer shares also, as he too sleeps, trusts, ages, and dies, watching always.

Upon rereading these texts, old and new, as they are inserted now in this present edition, one cannot help being conscious of the relationship of the figures in some composite imaginary picture, distant and yet intimate, unsentimental and yet of distinctly emotional affective power. The gray stone surrounding the scene is the background and yet is at the same time the stuff of which the figures are composed, legendary and yet actual, dead and yet living, suffering and imploring: the stone, by its wounding, offers its own cry of anguish. The night of imagination and dread is long and tormented, and the path seems interminable; the poems of this section end quietly, in separation, bareness, and indeterminate time, as the figures withdraw into loneliness.

"Le Chant de sauvegarde" ("The Song of Safe Conduct") returns to the figure of the Phoenix, to the scene of this death and shipwreck and passage by fire. Called by some bird cruel and of a black voice, the narrator enters, speaks, ages, and is silent, before hearing another song; as if an entire story were to have been absorbed in this short stanza. On a page alone we read or hear a song made of brief lines, telling both of destruction and salvation: "Que l'oiseau se déchire en sables, disais-tu, / Qu'il soit, haut dans son ciel de l'aube, notre rive" ("Let the bird tear apart in sand, you were saying / Let him be, high in his dawning sky, our shore," 129).

"Le Feuillage éclairé" ("The Foliage Lit"), which begins by an interrogation, is strengthened in this recent edition by the doubling of the question, "Dis-tu? Dis-tu?", conveying perfectly the feeling of legend, of vague mystery and certain sadness. It opens thus, after

the initial questions in their echoing repetition, leading into a
simplicity of statement consonant with the birdsong:

> Dis-tu qu'il se tenait sur l'autre rive,
> Dis-tu qu'il te guettait à la fin du jour?
>
> L'oiseau dans l'arbre de silence avait saisi
> De son chant vaste et simple et avide nos coeurs,
> Il conduisait
> Toutes voix dans la nuit où les voix se perdent (131)
>
> (Are you saying he stayed on the other shore,
> Are you saying he watched you closely at day's end?
>
> The bird in the tree of silence had seized our hearts
> With his vast, simple, and avid song
> He was leading
> All the voices in the night where voices are lost)

What we call after, as the bird well knows, is what is lost and is
to be found no more. Such a song is never unmixed with pain; again
we think of Rilke's bird song, joining inner and outer worlds, and
again of Baudelaire's Passerby, loved and lost, loved because lost.
The setting is full of memories, although bare of detail. With the
bird as guide, the wanderer in the lofty and tragic "boat laden with
grief" devotes himself to the task: "L'oiseau m'a appelé, je suis
venu" ("The bird called me, and I came," 130), and leaves what is
most familiar and homelike, the earth of lamplight and hearth, for
the night. The song was simple: presently it takes on a tone of irony
and a threat of death, while the vocabulary increasingly stresses
distance, refusal, blackness, poverty, and hardship; the bare moment
in the harsh work of earth.

The very harshness of the setting, while it sets the task and the
calling apart from the everyday, intensifies the solitude about the
one who, like Siegfried, will have now to seize the sword, bright-
colored with red and with blue, like a red sun against an azure sky,
or within the flame of some brightly colored fruits. For even in the
land of exile, the obscure land of shadow and yet of dawn, where
"une ombre essentielle / voile toute lumière et toute vérité" ("an
essential shadow / veils all light and all truth," 134), the love of
earth remains strong, and the love of love. The sun, rising only to

age and to sink, shares man's pattern. Each text will elaborate—although keeping the same simplicity—upon the hero's call, task, and knowledge. You (for the second-person form is retained) will hear the bird call, "like a sword in the distance," cutting through all the shadow and fear and despair, will see "shining the naked blade you must seize" (136), and this will be the end of waiting.

The task is legendary: the sword is cold, its handle rusty, and its flame now grown dark. It is inscribed in the stone, which bleeds from its wound, and on which the lessons of moving and dying are traced. The task is, as we might have expected, eternal, and endless. As other trees closed off the path after Douve's death and departure, these on the contrary open a path, which must be taken.

The concluding section, "À une Terre d'aube" ("To an Earth of Dawn") is brief. Its form is that of dedication, of a devotion as in the prose poem called by that name, at the end of the volume and already referred to: in this edition it has become a separate item, standing, as indeed it should, apart. Dawn, daughter of tears and suffering, is to rearrange and reshape the room of rest, and the heart to begin again and take on color, after that colorless face, in another brightness. Life will return afresh. "Écoute-moi revivre, je te conduis Au jardin de présence . . ." ("Hear me reliving, I lead you / To the garden of presence . . . ," 144). Each of a number of privileged images—the dawn coming, like the red wound of a sun against a sky, or water making a hollow in the stone of day, or fire and spirit seen in the broken bread, or the conflagration of every dead branch—discovers or uncovers a country. Again we think of the Heideggerian call and disclosure, in this "pays découvert" ("land discovered"). A star marks the threshold, and the ardor within is perhaps only what we call time. This is at last, then, the place, sought, toward which all steps were leading. "Le pas dans son vrai lieu" ("The step in its true place," 149). The voice after its unrest is happy in these rocks of silence, and will continue to sound within the stone of the tree, recalling another legendary task: Oedipus saved as well as sacrificed, about to do battle. For this voice: "The same voice, always," traverses all pain and anguish and all time, emanating from the bird of ruins.

Here, at the end of this yesterday which was deserted and was a desert *Hier régnant désert,* is the true, clear place, no longer dawn but now day, no longer the mirage of a song, but the certainty of the task chosen alone, in this place built from memory and from stone. "Ici, dans le lieu clair. . . . Ici, et jusqu'au soir. . . . Ici,

toujours ici" ("Here, in the clear place. . . . Here, and until evening. . . . Here, always here" 150).

The poetic path has not led far off, but only to a song of the here
and now, of a presence recaptured in full clarity.

From Stone to Threshold

Once more in *Pierre écrite (Written Stone)* as in *Du mouvement et de
l'immobilité de Douve,* an epigraph makes mention of death, but also,
now, of life, "Thou meetest with things dying; I with things new
born," from Shakespeare's *Winter's Tale.* Thus this volume is cast,
from the beginning, in a dialogue form between two attitudes. The
title: "the written stone," signifies at once a tombstone marking
the place of death, and an inscription made by a living hand, as on
a page, that page is hardened into durability. By its name, the
poem is thus incised in the memory and yet the name is also a
place—a *lieu-dit,* or familiar local spot. Thus, finally, the volume
is both universal and familiar.

The beginning section, "L'été de nuit" ("The Night Summer"),
is the reversal of another of Shakespeare's titles, *Midsummer Night's
Dream.* This nocturnal nine-part symphony is a reflection on starry
evenings, on privileged gardens and fruits, on darkness and lamps,
on light and ships, on a foliage "shining under the foliage," on
speech quiet in the sufficiency of summer and on stillness.

This latter concept also reminds us of *Douve,* and the tension
between immobility and movement therein, the motion of life and
its gestures, and the frantic gesticulations of dying before the motionlessness of death:

> Le mouvement
> Nous était apparu la faute, et nous allions
> Dans l'immobilité comme sous le navire
> Bouge et ne bouge pas le feuillage des morts. (165)

> (Movement
> Had seemed a fault to us, and we went
> In immobility as, under the ship,
> Moves and does not move the foliage of the dead.)

Here the beloved figure guiding the ship of living combines motion
and stillness in her gestures, as she leads the voyage, smiling; we
imagine here an antique smile in its ambiguity:

À jamais le reflet d'une étoile immobile
Dans le geste mortel.
Aimée, dans le feuillage de la mer. (165)

(Forever the reflection of a motionless star
In the mortal gesture.
Loved, in the foliage of the sea.)

As a red cloud will later guide the ship in *Dans le leurre du seuil,* here the figure is red-colored, and the shadows moving across her make patterns like the foliage. The elements of earth and sky and water are interpenetrating, the star attracted to the seafoam, and a clear path is made from the star to the ship's stern, in the tranquillity of water and summer and sky. Fitting into the summer peace, the line of verse runs smoothly, and is a statement of clarity:

Longtemps ce fut l'été. Une étoile immobile
Dominait les soleils tournants. L'été de nuit
Portait l'été de jour dans ses mains de lumière
Et nous nous parlions bas, en feuillage de nuit. (168)

(For a long time it was summer. A motionless star
Ruled the spinning suns. The night summer
Was bearing the day summer in its hands of light
And we spoke to each other softly, like foliage of night.)

Suns and stars, night and daylight and leaves are interwoven in this special season and setting. The sky seeks out the streams of earth for nourishment, "desirous and concerned," as it is in our image, and shares a light with us, and a night and a season. The summer itself, this privileged season, becomes the space traversed, like an unmoving ocean, leading to another, which will be endless.

In the ensuing poems, all part of one long poem in its changing lights and shades, the stars and sea are even closer, the stars taking our trees for their own, our garden walls for their fruits, and the sea extending its imagery until the stones of the mortal place carry a shadow into the "foam of the tree." Like the poems of Rimbaud in which land images merge with sea images (for instance, "Marine" or in a famous passage of Proust about ships, poppies, and a tapestry), the attributes of one element merge with those of another. The paths

of the sky cast their shadow on our earth, and on this song ship-
wrecked on our dark road, obscure and tinged with blood.

Not that such a statement is openly made: the face touched with
the "red mud of the dead" simply reminds us that the figure on
the prow was marked with red; the head bends over a beach where
death is glistening, as one water is lost in another, "in the redness
of somber water," and then, in the following poem, the dress will
be crimson.

Now interrupting the seminarrative thread with which I am trying
to link the texts, I should like to make a digression, to which
reference will be made once again in the final section on these poems,
describing figures and techniques. Since the point to be made is
most noticeably exemplified in these pages, I shall not try to separate
it from the present discussion: this color red, here associated with
blood and death, will later, in *Le Nuage Rouge,* be important also
for itself and not just as an attribute of the cloud. Colors in Bonnefoy's work are not exact in their coincidence with a face, or a body,
but carry a trace of feeling, identifiable to be sure with the figure—
yet not dependent exclusively upon it. Nor are they simply symbols:
each color matters in itself.

> .   .   .   ce visage taché
> De l'argile rouge des morts.
> ....
> Le signe de solitude
> Sur les pentes ocres d'un corps.
>
> Et telle une eau qui se perd
> Dans les rougeurs d'une eau sombre,
> La nuque proche se courbe
> Sur la plage où brille la mort. (174)
>
> (.   .   .   this face stained
> With the red mud of the dead.
> ....
> The sign of solitude
> On the ochre slopes of a body.
>
> And like a water losing itself
> In the redness of a somber water,
> The nearby nape bends over
> The beach where death glistens.)

As ochre stands in relation to redness, so solitude stands in relation
to death. But we must guard just as strongly against the idea that
red *symbolizes* death: the colors are no more purely symbolic than
they are simply descriptive: they have their own signifying power.

Thus for example, the lines in the poem following: "Solitude à
ne pas gravir, que de chemins! / Robe rouge, que d'heures proches
sous les arbres!" ("Loneliness not to be climbed, how many paths! /
Red dress, how many hours nearby under the trees!" 175). These
images associate once more loneliness with redness, but never make
a specific statement, never reduce this to that. And again,

> Le lieu des morts,
> C'est peut-être le pli de l'étoffe rouge.
> Peut-être tombent-ils
> Dans ses mains rocailleuses; s'aggravent-ils
> Dans les touffes en mer de la couleur rouge. . . . (185)

> (The place of the dead
> Is perhaps the pleat of red cloth.
> Perhaps they fall
> In its rugged hands; are made graver
> In the tufts of sea of a red color. . . .)

The reader can scarcely fail to think of the red garments of Christ's
passion, of the Red Sea, and perhaps of such poems as one of the
spiritial Théoremes de la Ceppède, where the red of the cloth becomes the red of Christ's flesh and of the red of his passion: ("To
conquering monarchs the red tunic / Belongs by right . . ."). But
the red here takes on its own character, unattached to any object
or sentiment it might "describe"—it has the hardness and the
enduring quality, in fact, of a stone, to be written upon, and with,
and about.

The stone as it speaks or is written has an enduring hardness, as
the water of being has depth and comports nourishment: "Dans le
boire éternel du jour plus bas que le jour" ("In the eternal drink of
the day lower than day," 179). Thus does poetry partake of both:
of the deep source and of the specific appearance. And the "Written
Stone" which forms the second part of the volume so entitled continues to stress the relation of sky to earth, as the stars measure out

the earthly surface of night, and mix with their own fires human
darkness, in response to human voices and human light, to lamps
and surrounding foliage: thus their word reaches us. As if in echo
of all the boats already glimpsed in Bonnefoy's work—in the poems,
in stories, in essays—and in preview of the others yet to come, the
small boats of the stars approach us. The repetition of the same few
images: ships and stars and summer, creates a vocabulary specific
to and powerful within the poem.

To take another example, directly following, the association of
the dead and their true place with the foliage gives an added sense
of human drama to the latter, familiar in Bonnefoy by its frequent
recurrence and patterning of dark against light, movement against
the static, like leaves against sky:

> Quel est le lieu des morts,
> Ont-ils droit comme nous à des chemins,
> Parlent-ils, plus réels étant leurs mots,
> Sont-ils l'esprit des feuillages ou des feuillages plus hauts? (183)

> (What is the place of the dead,
> Have they like us, a right to paths,
> Do they speak, their words being more real,
> Are they the spirit of the foliage or of some foliage higher?)

To the worlds of the living and the dead, the night renders us
more sensitive: so in this nocturnal atmosphere, the stones of memory and dead figures address us or each other or themselves: "Je fus
assez belle. / Il se peut qu'un jour comme celui-ci me ressemble"
("I was rather lovely. / It may be that a day like this one resembles
me," 184; "Deux ans, ou trois, / Je me sentis suffisante. / Les astres,
Les fleuves, les forêts ne m'égalaient pas" ("Two years before, or
three, / I felt myself sufficient. The stars, The streams, the forests
were not my equal," 186).

The poetry is solemn and yet simple, these stones, like tomb-
stones, reminding us of the past and yet—this is the strength of
the poetry—speaking as texts in the present. If the pictures in a
museum are placed there, in some sense, arbitrarily, they are still,
as Bonnefoy points out in his essay "On Painting and Place," meaningful also within and by that grouping. Just so, the gathering of
stones in a cemetery, or in the pages of this volume, is at once

unessential and essential, arbitrary and marvelous, each stone illuminated within the whole by its interrelations with the others.

Moreover, each individual memory and its particular passions can be deeply moving, no matter how common or how private the reference: "Qu'aurai-je aimé? L'écume de la mer / Au-dessus de Trieste . . ." ("What will I have loved? The sea foam / Above Trieste . . ." 191); or again: "J'ai lu longtemps le livre de Porphyre, / Je suis venu au lieu de nul soleil" ("I read at length the book of Porphyry, / I have come to the place of no sun," 193). The attachment of an individual reader, for instance, to a special place or connects author or thinkers that reader to the real, as words already do; the accidental and the arbitrary are so transfigured by their importance for the person speaking.

But now in this volume the day draws near, and though the boxwood is thick over the cemetery, like an old garden in its shadow, the dead stop speaking, their stones replaced by statues ("On an Eros of Bronze"), and by voices of the pagan world, enduring long after the cemetery figures have fallen silent. All of nature enters in the love—sun, shadow, life, age, foliage, dream, and death:

> Nous vieillissions, lui le feuillage et moi la source,
> Lui le peu de soleil et moi la profondeur,
> Et lui la mort et moi la sagesse de vivre.
>
> J'acceptais que le temps nous présentât dans l'ombre
> . . . .
> J'aimais, j'étais debout dans le songe éternel. (197)
>
> (We were aging, he the foliage and I the spring,
> He, the sparse sun and I the depth,
> He as death and I, the wisdom of living.
>
> I accepted time's presenting us in shadow
> . . . .
> I was in love, standing in the eternal dream.)

In "Un Feu va Devant Nous" ("A Fire Goes Ahead of Us"), the color red takes up once more its triumphal march, here clear and bright as passion ("La robe rouge éclairante" ["The red dress brightening," 199]), for the fire leads us here, as will the red cloud later.

The aggrandizement of images is especially to be noticed, for suddenly a shoulder becomes the dawn, and a body, a bright country "leaning over our shadows." Like the night drinking from the streams of the earth which we saw previously, the stature and expansiveness of the elements and figures of these poems retain this sense of a mythological landscape. The red dress—an object easily assimilated to everyday life—is here extended to become "Tout ce haut rougeoiement d'un impossible été" ("All this high reddening of an impossible summer," 200), and later, "Le rouge de la robe illumine et disperse / Loin, au ciel, le charroi de l'antique douleur" ("The red of the dress illumines and disperses / Far off, in the sky, the chariot of ancient pain," 201).

As a dress signifies an hour or a season, dawn (this fire before us) the time when lamplight loses its color before day, so the outer scene is also inner, and the heart is healed by the day's advent:

> Toi aussi tu aimes l'instant où la lumière des lampes
> Se décolore et rêve dans le jour.
> Tu sais que c'est l'obscur de ton coeur qui guérit,
> La barque qui rejoint le rivage et tombe. (201)

> (You too love the moment when the light of the lamps
> Grows faint of color and dreams in the day.
> You know your heart's darkness is healing,
> The boat which reaches the shore and falls.)

The fire, the dawn, the dress, all participate in redness and in the joy mixed with sorrow which is the mark of summer and the nostalgia felt for and within it. A time of intermingling, it lends itself also to the intensification of sentiment, to the realization of the other within the same: of aging within the unchanging, of the general vision beyond the specific: "L'arbre vieillit dans l'arbre, c'est l'été. / L'oiseau franchit le chant de l'oiseau et s'évade" ("The tree grows old within the tree, it is summer. / The bird traverses the song of the bird and escapes," 201). The *dépassement* or escape beyond has always been implicit in the dissipation of the present landscape; what lies further, or above or deeper, seems to be part of the reason for the vivid perception of the here and now:

Chemins, parmi
La matière des arbres. Dieux, parmi
Les touffes de ce chant inlassable d'oiseaux. (202)

(Paths, among
The matter of the trees. Gods, among
The tufts of this untiring birdsong.)

The beyond gives a significance to what is nearby and beloved in its familiarity: "Ô proche, ô tout mon jour" ("Oh near, oh all my day," 202), and nevertheless its interdependence with individual perception is experiential and singular. "Parfois je te savais la terre. . . . Parfois je te disais de myrte. . . . Ainsi je t'inventais parmi tes cheveux clairs" ("Sometimes I knew you to be the earth. . . . Sometimes I said you were of myrtle. . . . Thus I invented you among your fair hair," 203). It is to be observed that the verbs go in reverse order of certainty: knowing, saying without any guarantee of truth, and inventing. (The verb "inventer" can be taken, of course, also in its original sense of coming upon or finding, but in combination with saying "as if," and directly preceding a reference to dream, the invention or the vision seems consonant with the schema just established, stretching from certainty to imagination.) All the action takes place in a bed likened to a free boat, putting out to sea, a contrapuntal echo to the previous boat of stars as it touches land.

But the red color now reappears in a text where there converge blood, a lively flame and a red material; the convergence is resonant as the blood is "unappeased," but abundantly positive in the following poem, where the fruit is crimson in the sun. Evening falls, birds chatter in the blue and black streaks like ploughed furrows in the sky, while the human figures remain, in a painting bright with color and silent in the fading light:

Nous sommes immobiles depuis longtemps.
Nous parlons bas.
Et le temps reste autour de nous comme des flaques de couleur. (207)

(We have been motionless for a long time.
We speak softly.
And time remains around us like pools of color.)

The colors are not here finally attached to the elements, but are
separate, signifying only themselves, as each of the lines is end-
stopped by a period.

In this "hour with the open arches" (208), the spacious stillness
and openness seem on one hand empty, and on another, brightness
incarnate: "this time deserted and full of day" (208); the figures are
solemn, yet devoid of sadness. There are no useless details, no details
in fact at all, no reference to time past or future. The present, like
color as I am discussing it here, is exactly *coincident* with itself and
needs no projection beyond:

> Combien simples, oh fûmes-nous, parmi ces branches
> ....
> Je t'avais converti aux sommeils sans alarmes,
> Aux pas sans lendemains, aux jours sans devenir
> ....
> À de grands chemins clos, où venait boire l'astre
> Immobile d'aimer, de prendre et de mourir. (209)
>
> (How simple, oh, we were among these branches
> ....
> I had converted you to sleeping free of fright,
> To steps with no morrow, to days without becoming
> ....
> To great closed paths, where there came to drink
> The motionless star of loving, taking, and dying.)

The actions are large and generalized, like love and nourishment
and death, accomplished by what one imagines as continuous gestures, devoid of the jerkiness that our more specific acts can betray.

In this way, I think, a stone would speak, or a nonpersonalized
voice, never tied down by a proper name or memory. A fire is still
leading us ("Un feu va devant nous," 210) and yet the scene will
now change to the darker side, to an "obscure festival" celebrated
in the evening dusk and ashes, detached from the brightness of the
flame. The lighting has altered, the scene has shifted, nor are the
attributes of the figures constant:

> Nous ne nous voyons plus dans la même lumière,
> Nous n'avons plus les mêmes yeux, les mêmes mains.
> L'arbre est plus proche et la voix des sources plus vive,

Nos pas sont plus profonds, parmi les morts. (211)

(We no longer see in the same light,
We have no longer the same eyes, the same hands.
The tree is nearer and the voice of the springs livelier,
Our steps are deeper, among the dead.)

The steps once taken on the surface of the ground are now sinking deeper to death. With human anguish the stars come again to mingle, and with the trees and the birdsongs, the shadows, and the days of shifting light.

Here we sense the echo of the negative theology referred to in the preface to the essays of *L'Improbable:* the God who is not is to be renounced in us as we are to be erased in him, these cancellations of identity compared to a "fruit splitting apart." From here to the discovery of a mysterious meaning in what is "only simple," there is but a brief step. This changed light is itself one of the more meaningful titles: "La Lumière, Changée": the change of illumination and of depth brings a new feeling to the poetry, and the words of which it, and love, are made. The tone of interrogation adds greatly to this increased sense of renewed and accumulated depth; a stone, speaking, questions and answers also:

Le jour au fond du jour sauvera-t-il
Le peu de mots que nous fûmes ensemble?
Pour moi, j'ai tant aimé ces jours confiants, je veille
Sur quelques mots éteints dans l'âtre de nos coeurs. (212)

(The day at day's depth will it save
The few words that we were together?
Myself I have so loved these confident days, I watch
Over a few words extinguished in the hearth of our hearts.)

Speech, through its strong concretion, has taken on new density and darkness: these are sober words, whose weight is felt against the most sad or thoughtful hands, and which warm even the most mournful paths of evening, giving off heat at their very core. Words— and art—provide the only real radiance acknowledged by the poet, comprise the lamp he holds, in its redness, as metaphor against age and death: here again the color has taken the place of any descriptive adjective and stands alone, as the essence of motion: "Et toi, mon rougeoiement de lampe dans la mort" ("And you, my reddening of lamp in death," 215). The ship wandering is brought, too, to brightness, seen as a "clarity of nearby night and clarity of word": the far is rendered near at days' end.

And the section concludes with earthly happiness and peace, compared to some "irregular" insect cry—as imperfect as the summit called for in the poetic work ("L'imperfection est la cime")— for the irregular seems endowed with a greater emotional power than the regular. All around, silence, rising in a wind from the book to the heart among the fruition and the fullness of a time without complication, of an aging without menace, seen simply as a loss of color in the trees and no trace of violence:

> Simples dans le verger sont les fruits mûrs.

> Tu vieilliras
> Et, te décolorant dans la couleur des arbres,
> Faisant ombre plus lente sur le mur. . . . (217)

> (Simple in the orchard are the ripe fruits.

> You will age
> And, your color fading in the color of trees,
> Making a slower shadow on the wall. . . .)

Clarity abounds, and meaning, so that the conclusion ties together book and speech, brightness and dark, future and past. You will find, says the poet at the end of the text just quoted, "Le Livre, pour vieillir" ("The Book, For Growing Old"), that these were the last obscure words. As if writing were to finish—perhaps it is the case—with understanding.

The final section, "Le Dialogue d'Angoisse et de Désir" ("The Dialogue of Anguish and of Desire," 219), retains the fruits and the evening setting of the last texts just seen, in an understated surprise at the passing of time and its effort, and at the reassembling power of speech, in its ancient vocabulary and the new. Ripening within the garden where we are placed, what we have suffices for us, in this time grown simple. The dialogue is followed at a slow pace throughout the pages, always in the tone of acceptance, in the fullness of seasons.

Et je m'étonne alors qu'il ait fallu
Ce temps, et cette peine. Car les fruits
Régnaient déjà dans l'arbre. Et le soleil
Illuminait déjà le pays du soir.

....

Toute l'âme se voûte autour d'un dire simple,
La grisaille se perd dans le fruit mûr.

....

Nous n'avons plus besoin
D'images déchirantes pour aimer.
Cet arbre nous suffit là-bas. . . . (219–21)

(And I am surprised then that it took
This time, and this toil. For the fruits
Were already reigning in the tree. And the sun
Was already lighting the land of evening.

....

The whole soul is vaulted around a simple speech,
The greyness is lost in the ripe fruit.

....

We have no further need
Of heartrending images to love.
That tree over there is enough for us. . . .)

The gardens once obscure are illuminated, like the words, light lingers over the earth, after a day of distinct color, uncomplicated and clear: "Et nous avons vielli un peu. Et le bonheur / A mûri ses fruits clairs en d'absentes ramures" ("And we have grown a little older. / And happiness has ripened its bright fruits in absent branches," 223). Distance is changed to nearness, instead of waiting, the present hour suffices, and once more the general is brought within the personal, in lines of quiet assurance quite unlike any others in contemporary French poetry:

. . . Les fruits anciens
Soient notre faim et notre soif enfin calmées.
Le feu soit notre feu. Et l'attente se change
En ce proche destin, cette heure, ce séjour. (224)

(. . . May the ancient fruits
Be our hunger and our thirst calmed at last.
May the fire be our fire. And waiting changes
To this nearby fate, this hour, this sojourn.)

After such a beginning, as it is stated, and in "the same place" of
the mortal earth, the conclusion is perfect. For here at last the seen
and the felt are mingled, and each work of art—as here Tintoretto's
Pietà, comes into its own in human life, becoming, as surely as the
landscape, a part of the here and the now.

Human desire, vivified in its turn by the art image, or by the
poetic voice, contributes to the *ars poetica* of the final text, where
the human voice in its suffering is washed and redeemed, called
back *(rappelé)* into the text. As the clear language has, says a voice,
consumed the poet, he himself enters, by means of this fiery consumption of words, the universe around, impersonal and personal,
its monuments and its empty spaces, its figures, its radiance and
its revelation:

> Je suis cet autel vide, et ce gouffre, et ces arches
> Et toi-même peut-être, et le doute: mais l'aube
> Et le rayonnement de pierres descellées. (226)

> (I am this empty altar, and this chasm, and these arches
> And yourself perhaps, and doubt; but dawn
> And the radiance of unsealed stones.)

In *Dans le leurre du seuil* (In the Lure of the Threshold) the epigraph
is again from *A Winter's Tale,* and again, it opposes the contraries
as in *Pierre écrite,* where the epigraph from the same play opposed
dying to being born ("Thou meetest with things dying; I with
things new born"), or the one for *Hier regnant désert* taken from
Hölderlin: "You have everything and you have nothing," or Hegel's
concept of life supporting death in *Douve;* "They looked as they had
heard of a world ransom'd, or one destroyed," begins this present
volume. As the dichotomy is immediately set up, the universe is
given its initial structure by two great abstractions, then filled in
by subsequent details in the working out.

This volume, however, is unlike the preceding ones in several
ways instantly perceptible. It is not made up of separate voices and
the voices of stones, not, therefore, structured by a series of oral
and inscribed sayings. It is rather one long poem, interrupted occasionally by a line of suspension marks, indicating ellipsis, that
is, both interruption and continuity. So also, the subtitles could be
read like the titles of landscape paintings, separate and yet in series:

"The River," "In the Lure of the Threshold," "Two Colors and Two Boats," "The Earth," "The Clouds," "The Scattered," "The Indivisible." If I name them now, before any sequential discussion of the text, it is in order to have them seen in their set and setting, with River, Earth, and Clouds responding, with the pair of boats echoing the pair of colors, and the oxymoronic title at the conclusion of this work, whose elements are scattered but inseparable in thought, whose spirit participates both in the rending apart and the resuming of the universe.

The river and the river gods, the mythological place of crossing, the stream of consciousness and of language, all of these open this volume, which, among all of Bonnefoy's work may be considered the most majestic, at once continuous and dense, flowing as the river and variable in its currents. A pause of thirteen years separates this publication from that of *Pierre écrite,* so it is not altogether surprising that a change has occurred.

The difference is less one of style, however, than of substance; in spite of the noticeable stylistic differences from the texts on which I have previously commented. Or then, a change in the felt presence of the poet: a great subtlety remains, but quiet, a rounding off of some edges, but not to the point of bluntness, a deepening of the emotions felt by speaker and reader, but not toward the easily sentimental. As one might expect, such an indivisible volume is far harder to comment upon in its own order, to "narrate" in its flow, in short, to present, than the former volumes where the inner divisions were clearly marked.

Still here, after this thirteen-year interval, the season of summer obsesses above all others. The gestures have even more the appearance of the everlasting than in *Douve;* the gaze of the observer is focused upon the creation at once specific, localizable in an instant, and given an extension into infinity by haunting memory and visionary prediction: "Et tu te lèves une éternelle fois / Dans cet été qui t'obsède" ("And you rise one eternal time / In this summer obsessing you," 231). It may always be summer when a figure rises thus, hearing a sound of an elsewhere, "near, far": both in time and space the present is extended and projected. This, as I have tried to point out in previous commentaries, is one effect of the reduction of details and figures and elements to a very few, so that the gaze is focused upon one spot, the energy gathered and conserved for that later projection: "Look!" the poet cries, and the reiteration of the command acts also upon the reader, whose vision is thus captured, constrained, and guided.

The major object before the eyes is the river as it runs, uniting the stars with the mortal fruits, however "vainly." For an incurable wound separates the lasting sparkle from the obscurity of our lives. They are given their continuity by our ancient and familiar mythology (a boat leaving a riverbank, Charon rowing the dead across the river Lethe, the place of forgetting), and by our nostalgia for a such a legendary time:

> Ô terre, terre,
> Pourquoi la perfection du fruit, lorsque le sens
> Comme une barque à peine pressentie
> Se dérobe de la couleur et de la forme,
> Et d'où ce souvenir qui serre le coeur
> De la barque d'un autre été au ras des herbes? (233)

> (Oh earth, earth,
> Why the perfection of the fruit, when meaning
> Like a boat scarcely sensed
> Slips away from color and from form,
> Whence comes this memory which grips the heart
> Of the boat of another summer level with the grass?)

Another question lingers, about certainty and even joy, in spite of this enigma: why does the image—neither appearance nor dream—persist in spite of the "denial of being?" These are profound days, peopled with figures as of some Poussin painting, with their costumes and slow gestures somehow larger than life: images more than symbols, but communicating to the text itself a largeness in no way explicable by the presumed content of the gestures:

> . . . Jours profonds,
> Un dieu jeune passait à gué le fleuve,
> Le berger s'éloignait dans la poussière,
> Des enfants jouaient haut dans le feuillage,
> Rires, batailles dans la paix, les bruits du soir,
> Et l'esprit avait là son souffle, égal. . . (233)

> (. . . Profound days,
> A young god was crossing the river,
> The shepherd went off into the dust,

> Children were playing high in the foliage,
> Laughter, struggling in the peace, the sounds of evening,
> And the spirit there breathed evenly. . . .)

The figures are made the quintessence of what they are and do, are placed at the limits of possible meaning: into them can be read all one wants to read, and yet they would suffice, free of anything other than themselves. Never before, says the text, and the implication is absolute: never again, never more than this, never like this: never have more violent stars been seen, never has a wilder call of a shepherd been heard, never this, in any summer so dark and so obscure.

That is the setting for the work, described in a long-line verse befitting the calm of this canvas and its innate intensity, but then suddenly and severely shortened in the section which gives its title to the volume, beginning with the harshness of a striking gesture, as riveting as the word "Look!" Here we read: "Heurte!" ("Strike!" or then "Knock!"), into the lure of the threshold. The force of the command is heightened by the contrast of these peremptory lines with the previous smoothness of the river's flow. Like a knock upon a door whose sound is muffled and does not project into the distance, the action stops short. The sound of the word "fer" evokes only "iron," and not, for example, some symbolized constructive hardness or a joy in creation; the word "fer" might, for instance, evoke, as it often does, the verb "faire" or "to make," or some implication of a cast-iron monument. In this universe of uselessness and absence, of dryness and extinction, the ferryman will mediate for us, but not settle us in any position too hard or too sure.

The human voice is rejected by the wind of words, tearing apart our work; even the beloved figures are unapproachable, their rooms empty of all but the self calling the other, now deeply prey to the doubt previously sensed. The violence of the images betrays the sudden emptiness: the dark beak of an eagle rends his own chest, and nothingness spurts forth. This appears to be the dark chaos before the creation of light and the world: both are contained in the lines preceding two rows of suspension marks, the form of prechaos and precreation parallel to the thought, these lines perched on the edge of an abyss marked thus formally in the text:

> . . . Dehors,
> C'est encore le temps de la douleur
> Avant l'image.
> Dans la main de dehors, fermée,
> A commencé à germer
> Le blé des choses du monde. (252)
>
> (. . . Outside,
> It is still the time of pain
> Before the image.
> In the hand of outside, closed,
> There has begun to sprout
> The wheat of the things of this world.)

After the bare description of that empty and dark world, "Deux couleurs" ("Two Colors") begins with two human hands possessing nothing but their own confidence. Life, were it to arise, would have to start with only this dream of a possible beginning. In the river's smooth surface, a sky can be awakened, and a tree of stars, and eventually another life. Sleeping in the naked potential of the dark water are worlds, summer nights, leaves, human and animal signs, or their reflections to be reflected on. And, as in Poussin's canvas *Moses Saved from Drowning* which Bonnefoy mentions in *L'Arrière-Pays,* essence and meaning and possibility are given by the most modest images, an initiating small figure carrying the weight and the promise of what is to be: "Plus avant que l'étoile / Dans ce qui est / Se baigne simple l'enfant / Qui porte le monde" ("Further on than the star / In what is / The child bearing the world / Is bathing, simply," 258). The two colors of the title are his, a blue which takes on a greenness from the treetops (as a fire becomes bright, says the poet, among the fruits), and the deep red of the heavy painted cloth that the Egyptian women were washing in the river by night: Poussin's red, Poussin's blue, and the forming of a world to come. This long poem has something of the germ of creation in it, and the certainty of a universe about to be.

"Deux Barques" ("Two Ships") initially presents two beings willing to put off their personalities and distinctions in order to begin at zero in creation: thus the plea of one to the other: "Fais que je n'aie pas de visage, pas de nom" ("Cause me to have no face, no name," 261). Accept, says the first one, the indifferentiation of pure being, so that, like God and blind, I may embrace namelessness in embracing you in the night. This voluntary exile from identity will be, then, the origin of being, in a proved selflessness. Like a pagan baptism, the ritual of a new start requires only the essential, water as it provides forgetfulness of the past and a fresh possibility after the death of the old self: "Eau qui fait que nous sommes, n'étant pas" ("Water that causes us to be, not being," 262). The troubling of the water once more mingles the original with the reflection and casts doubt upon the doubling, the invention, and even, perhaps, upon the fable of the new creation. And as after the chaos and emptiness there was creation, now after the doubt, there appear the space and the plenty of summer:

> Paix, sur l'eau éclairée. On dirait qu'une barque
> Passe, chargée de fruits. . . .
> Paix, sur le flot qui va. Le temps scintille. (265–66)

> (Peace, upon the water brightened. You would say a ship
> Was passing, laden with fruit. . . .
> Peace, upon the water moving. Time is gleaming.)

A red light—like dawn in the preceding volumes, like the red dress, the red cloud—rustles in the pleats of the dress—this red light comes from the lap of a servant lighting the way, as a flowering almond tree shows us the profusions of the natural universe, before the dawn of the newest day.

"La Terre" ("The Earth") rediscovers what was, but now transfigured, the same language but unified, the same simplicity and bare minimality, but—as in the first title—with the elements reassembled and endowed with new meaning: "Look!" the command comes again, and this time, we look, but perceive differently:

> Je crie, Regarde,
> La lumière
> Vivait là, près de nous! Ici, sa provision
> D'eau, encore transfigurée. Ici le bois
> Dans la remise. Ici, les quelques fruits
> A sécher dans les vibrations du ciel de l'aube.

> Rien n'a changé,
> Ce sont les mêmes lieux et les mêmes choses,
> Presque les mêmes mots,
> Mais, vois, en toi, en moi

L'indivis, l'invisible se rassemblent. (271–274)

(I cry, Look,
The light
Was living there, near us! Here, its provision
Of water, transfigured still. Here, the wood
In the shed. Here, the few fruits
For drying in the vibrations of the dawn sky.

Nothing has changed,
These are the same places and the same things,
Nearly the same words,
But see, in you, in me
The undivided, the invisible are met.)

Consenting to the universe thus re-created, to the images of love:
the flowering almond-tree, the flame celebrating and consuming,
and to the minimal details of everyday life thus transformed: "Notre
chambre de l'autre année, mystérieuse / Comme la proue d'une
barque qui passe" ("Our room from the other year, mysterious /
Like the prow of a passing ship," 274). All these simple things are
here "reestablished," reinstituted in the light, and higher up, in a
place—a true place—of abundance, and of "pure naked presence /
on the bed of morning and the bed of evening" (270). Each stretching
toward the other, humans bend over, and the voices once interrupted
rise again. Now the sky is faintly red, the stones of the evening are
lit, and the cry of joy remains questioning, lingering as if in the
consent reiterated and of the identification of the narrator and the
thing perceived. "I the cloud / I consent. I the evening-star / I
consent."

The poet as baptizer, as narrator—becomes the ferryman of a
poetic boat, "of everything through everything."

"The Nuées" ("The Clouds") shows, in longer lines, the harmonious relation of clouds to each other as if in a musical piece, or
in the conclusion of a play when each recognizes each, and discovers,
as in A *Winter's Tale*, "a world redeemed and a world lost." The
clouds indicate presence, nearness, the readiness of the universe now
to be lived in: "Tout n'est-il pas si cohérent, si prêt / Bien que
certes, scellé?" ("Isn't everything coherent and ready / Although

surely sealed?" 294). But the ship's goal is not yet reached, and the misery of meaning has not healed.

A black spot haunts every image and a cry pierces every musical harmony, and all the hope of reassembling and unity cannot bring about the transfiguration dreamed of, whose outline the poet has sketched, knowing that our true place is not yet come.

The text is broken at this point, and thus matches all the unfinished images and the dream not realized. Here, says the poet, the task I know not how to complete, the words I shall not say, the blind spot in the gaze. "Look," indeed, and the gaze is fixed upon the light of evening on the windows, upon the red boat passing, upon the vine with its promise of fruit. We know, of course, that the light of the window will be extinguished sooner or later, that the summer which now absorbs our attention will disappear, and yet the *evidence* is near at hand:

> Mais que ce jour est clair!
>   . . . tout cela
> Dit la vie enfin prête à soi et non la mort.
> Vois, il aura suffi de faire confiance . . . (305)

> (But how bright is this day!
>   . . . all that
> Tells of life at last ready for itself and not of death.
> See, confidence will have been enough . . .

The word is unfinished, as is being itself, but its joy can now "take form". The images are appropriately ambiguous and still luminous: the water held in its vessel, however fugitive, the fire reflected, although basically made of nothing, the red cloud and the earth and sky, dotted as far as the eye can reach with red stones traced with what may be signs.

No certainty is possible, or desired: the evening sky is silent above us, like a bridge caved in. Here the personal reference is suggestive: a certain countryside, resembling language, and the few stones taken home, their redness burning the figures who carry them. Still, the summer, still the star on the threshold, for the dwelling the reader can only suppose.

"L'Épars, l'indivisible" ("The Sparse, the Indivisible") concludes the volume with a resounding series of affirmations and conjectures, in spite of time:

> Oui, par la voix
> Violente contre le silence de,
> Par le heurt de l'épaule
> Violemment contre la distance de
> —Mais de ta foudre d'indifférence tu partages,
> Ciel soudain noir,
> Le pain de notre solitude sur la table. (313)

> (Yes, by the voice
> Violent against the silence of,
> By the shock of the shoulder
> Violently against the distance of
> —But with the thunder of indifference you share,
> Sky suddenly black,
> The bread of our solitude upon the table.)

Yes, declares the poet, by the hand and the day and the sky and even by the hardened salt, time-stricken, by all this, I give my oath.

And this place, covered over with brambles and "the ashes of a hope" speaks of a desire consumed already: "Car nous aurons vécu si profond les jours / Que nous a consentis cette lumière!" ("For we shall have lived so deeply the days / Which this light has granted us!" 316–17). This is a picture of any dwelling, as the sky with reddening stones on one side and a light increasing might be that of any sky, as the red dress glimpsed might be any dress, the threshold with its broken arch, any threshold. Its missing stone might be found anywhere at all. That the poet has a particular dwelling, dress, sky, threshold in mind does not limit the poem, or close it off to us.

Now a fruit is held out, a boat turns red in the evening light, a fiery sun is reflected on the water, and on a silent afternoon, "Le temps dort dans la cendre du feu d'hier" ("time sleeps in the ashes of yesterday's fire," 321). The wasp knocking into the window has already healed the rent made in the world by the absence of meaning, as the smallest natural event can cure the metaphysical wound inflicted by abstract thought, the conceptual malady healed by the humblest "real" thing. The window itself is no longer a separating element, distancing what is seen from the one seeing, but rather the mediation between outer and inner, bringing the mind near to the object and vice versa:

> Et à ses vitres les feuillages sont plus proches
> Dans des arbres plus clairs. Et reposent les fruits
> Sous l'arche du miroir. Et le soleil
> Est haut encore, derrière la corbeille
> De l'été sur la table et des quelques fleurs. (322)

> (And in its panes the foliage is nearer
> In brighter trees. And the fruits rest
> Under the arch of the mirror. And the sun
> Is still high, behind the basket
> Of summer on the table and of a few flowers.)

The feeling of peace in the accumulation of simple riches is intensified by the tripled "Et" (whose sound is taken up once more in the "est" and the "été"), until it is heard seven times in this same stanza, calling attention to the profusion of clarity and brightness in close proximity to the speaker, to the height and transparency of the setting as well as the reflection, and to the gestures of offering, the basket appearing all the more abundant for the metonymy or ellipsis: the basket of summer, instead of the "basket of summer fruits," the latter arriving only afterward to fill the summery container. All possible ripeness is included in the summer light proferred upon the table, its abundance standing in formal opposition to the few flowers. Mirror and sun, fruits and flowers, tree and leaves, basket and table; the elements stand out in their very bareness of description (what kind of flowers? what sort of basket? of table? what fruits? what colors of flowers, of fruits, of basket, or trees?) The lighting is both clear and near. The still life is a good one, and convincing; were we to look back at the *vanitas* with the death's skull of *L'Anti-Platon,* with which it makes a perfect contrast, bright and joyous against dark and ominous, ordered and profuse against disheveled and stark, we would see Bonnefoy's poetry set in a fitting frame: death to life, end to beginning, and peculiar to simple. The *oui* which begins and ends this volume finally answers as only it can, the implicit initial question of the *Anti-Platon* about life and death, acceptance and refusal, and answers positively.

The means of salvation is also simple: not a whole vocabulary, but a few words, "saved / For a child's mouth." The complicated things and images can be stacked away among the "stones," said by other "voices" (filed away in the pages written and forgotten, of so many "pierres écrites"). The rights of and the right to a simpler dream and reality too are asserted against the overblown and over-ambitious wishes of reestablishing a meaning, of restoring a real luminosity to "the wounded word of light" (324) and of the vain effort to build, for we have only a "brief earth": this "terre brève" is again an ellipsis and a telescoping: brief life, small earth held in the narrow space of a poem.

Writing has a limited goal but a sufficient one, which extends beyond the traditional one of making specific and thereby possessing what is spoken of: "La douleur de nommer parmi les choses / Finira" ("The pain of naming among things / Will finish," 323). To deliver and to reassure, to bring peace, and to bring together what has been separate:

> Que la beauté,
> Car ce mot a un sens, malgré la mort,
> Fasse oeuvre de rassemblement de nos montagnes
> Pour l'eau d'été, étroite,
>
> Et l'appelle dans l'herbe,
> Prenne la main de l'eau à travers les routes,
> Conduise l'eau d'ici, minime, au fleuve clair. (325)
>
> (May beauty,
> For this word has meaning, despite death,
> Work to reassemble our mountains
> For summer's narrow water,
>
> And call it to the grass,
> May it take water's hand across the roads,
> Leading the least water from here to the clear river.)

Yes, says the poet, "by the hand I take / Upon this earth," and thus the vow to living here and now is made. The consent is also a witness borne. The stream to be forded among the stones, the books dreamed of, whose pages are turned by fire, the most broken of voices and the most modest of joys, all of these are everywhere and make part of the promise and the acceptance: "Par hier, réin-carné, ce soir, demain / Oui, ici, là, ailleurs, ici, là-bas encore"

("By yesterday reincarnate, tonight, tomorrow, / Yes, here, there, elsewhere, here, over there again," 327). The poem has expanded to fill the heavens, and is concentrated in the smallest place, the shortest moment:

> Les mots comme le ciel,
> Infini,
> Mais tout entier dans la flaque brève. (329)

> (Words like the heaven,
> Infinite,
> But entire in the brief pool.)

So the book ends also with all its own expansion concentrated in the modest pool on the page, situated, paradoxically and therefore perfectly and imperfectly, in a written stone.

From Song to Understanding

Song and Silence.   In the passage we take guided by the voices and stories (various, but also parts of each other) of Bonnefoy's poetry, we follow two seemingly contrary psychological directions. First, an apparent crescendo: from the part to the whole, or from the disconnected expression to the unifying word or phrase, the movement being always interior to the sense and never a question of volume. On the most elementary level, the two lines following, taken from the early *Douve,* can be read as a microcosmic model of the path we follow throughout the entire work: "Et je vous appartiens par son cheminement / À travers tant de nuit et malgré tout ce fleuve" ("And I belong to you by her path taken / Across so much night and despite all this river" *DM,* 67). Even the part here ("je vous ap*parti*ens") is phonetically included in the whole of the path, as is the "vers" ("à tra*vers*") in the crossing. In the balanced appositional structure characteristic of the poet, the *et* of the second line symmetrically separates the first half from the second, so that the expressions respond as double to double: "tant . . . tout / de . . . ce / nuit . . . fleuve." A progression is clear: from the partial "tant" to the complete "tout," from the neutral "de" to the specific and foregrounding "ce," from the obscurity of natural darkness in "nuit" to the continuity of the "fleuve," an image strong enough to bear the verbal and symbolic weight of the long path, the "chemine-

ment," and placed in exactly the same position within the verse
structure as the night, and equally stressed.

We might compare with this another line, in a poem whose title,
"Hic est locus patriae" ("Here is the place of the country"), calls
attention to the here of the text as the place of our belonging:
"C'était jour de parole et ce fut nuit de vent" ("It was a day of word
and a night of wind," *DM,* 102).

Here the balance is set up, with an initial contrast between a
slow descriptive imperfect tense and a more rapid and precise pre-
terite tense: "c'était . . . ce fut / jour . . . nuit / parole . . .
vent." Again the binary oppositions of the first two sets of elements
lead to the odd parallel contrast of the last one: the underlying basis
for the joining of speech and wind is the classic link of the breath
to the soul: *souffle* and *anima,* and we remember that in Bonnefoy's
thought, "the word is the soul of what it names."

The second direction apparent in this reading, opposite to the
crescendo, is that of a reduction, signaled repeatedly in the form as
well as the sense. In "Rive d'une autre mort" ("Shore of another
Death"), the bird grown weary of his role as Phoenix gradually
undoes himself and his myth in the depths of misery, through a
four-step progression shaped like a sonnet, and to which I have
already referred, each step leading into a stanza: "L'oiseau se défera
par misère profonde . . . / Il vieillira . . . / Il se taira . . . / Il
saura bien mourir . . ." ("The bird will undo himself through deep
suffering . . . / He will age . . . / He will be silent . . . / He
will know how to die . . . ," *DM,* 136). The slow acquisition of
this last knowledge seems to come, like the comprehension in *L'Arrière-Pays,* through the progression itself of the undoing and the
path toward another place, for this poem ends by "l'autre monde
obscur" ("the other dark world").

In the next part of this same series human voices, falling silent,
replace the voice of the bird no longer rearising as the Phoenix;
both these negative images follow positive beginnings. The uttering
of useless words is questioned, in the face of night, and the alter-
native is preferred, being no speech at all. "Nous n'aurons pas parlé"
("We shall not have spoken," DM, 137). This final silence permits
another landscape to emerge like the coast of a new understanding,
described now in a language inaccessible to the speaker: "la côte
longtemps vue et dite par des mots que nous ne savions pas" ("the
coast, for a longtime seen and said by words we did not know").

A preceding poem, "Lieu du combat" ("Place of Combat"), has prepared the resonance of this one, and in the undoing for an unspoken rebirth: "Voici défait le chevalier de deuil. . . . / Il se tait. . . . / Il se tait . . ." ("Here, is the knight of sorrow undone. . . . / He keeps silent. . . . / He keeps silent. . . ," *DM*, 219).

The bird's quiet responds to the repeated reticence of the knight of sorrow, and it is at the heart of this quiet, surrounded moreover, by a "dead sound," that the voice here speaking will be lost until the birth of the other song "qui s'éveille / Au fond désert du chant de l'oiseau qui s'est tu" ("awaking / In the desert depth of the birdsong which has fallen still," *DM*, 159). The Phoenix is not vanquished forever, not even unheard: it will be nourished on silence itself.

Formally, this movement of decline, down the page from the poem's beginning to its end, would seem to answer to a poetic attitude where the ending of the word is privileged. The movement is complicated by the interplay of words, where by homophony one indicates another, or others whose intensity echoes and builds on its own. Minor examples of this can be readily cited: for instance, in a doubling already seen elsewhere, the *fer* or iron of the bird corresponds to the poetic voice by the rereading *faire* or "make," the sword of his voice meeting the travail of the poet's work, and by extension, his silence joining with the silence of the poet, in contrast with the other voices of other texts. Or again, in the first of the four texts we shall briefly consider in a moment, the *mais* ("but") read as *mets* ("place") in conjunction with the words "étends . . . tes nappes" ("stretch out . . . your cloths"), in a parallel of the form with the image of a cloth laid down like a *toile de fond*, a backdrop for this poetry and its reflection on itself.

To see a working out of these structures as they give possible support to this verbal line moving toward silence, we may consider four texts in the order in which they appear in this early volume. It must be stated from the beginning that the repeated sound *e*, which by implication signals all the occurrences of the *et* ("and") of apposition, as do the frequently exact repetitions, "ici . . . ici," "ô . . . ô," "J'ai . . . J'ai," would seem to be further indications of progression and extension, in opposition to any real decline.

Across the cloth extended as a backdrop, the play of such words as "sombre / ombre" ("somber / shadow"), where the second is in-

cluded in the first, is like another tree within the tree, or birdsong
within the birdsong, to use Bonnefoy's images. If the deictic repetition: "ici . . . ici ("here . . . / here") marks an intense consciousness of place, of situation and scene, the rapidly building
positive crescendo within this poem ("étends . . . insinue . . .
viens . . . avance . . . et chante . . . souris, et chante") will be
placed finally in contrast with the somber light of its conclusion,
and the apparently negative ending:

> Et chante. C'est pleurer deux fois ce que tu pleures
> Si tu oses chanter par grand refus.
> Souris, et chante. Il a besoin que tu demeures,
> Sombre lumière, sur les eaux de ce qu'il fut. (D, 110)

> (And sing. You weep twice for what you weep for
> If you dare to sing in great refusing.
> Smile, and sing. He needs you to remain,
> Somber light, on the waters of what he was.)

In the following text, already quoted, the repeated question about
place and identity, "Où es-tu, qui es-tu?" marks another scene, this
one psychologically uncertain, where the voice speaking is swallowed
up, as if in the past of these waters "of what he was." The conclusion
of each step within the poem increases the impossibility of motion
forward, catching every move in a static repetition: "even this respite," "even lost." The stress laid on the past of being and action,
"ce qu'il *fut*," is by the echo of the "fut" already in apposition with
the words "je me suis *perdu*" and the concluding "qui s'est tu" of
one of the texts said by "Une voix," as well as the poem for Kathleen
Ferrier, "un chant qui s'est *perdu*." The potential loss of voice—
that of the bird, of the speaker, and of the singer—matches the
actual loss of action and presence. The word "perdu" acts, in all
these texts, as the continuous base, heard or sensed, against which
the rest resounds, diminished and deprived of light: the garden with
its brambles of memory overgrown, and the tears first radiant and
then swallowed up by the water of the poem, itself somber like the
countryside roadless and the steps without motion.

Now in a rereading, the last line of the first text, "Sombre
lumière, sur les eaux de ce qu'il fut," finds its response not only in
the deserted depth of the bird song, quiet and mythless, and in the
dead singer's voice lost forever to us, but more gravely, in the

darkness of the last line quoted: "cygne, lieu réel dans l'irréel eau sombre." The somber waters are directly preceded, in this long path of a long poem, by the somber light, an oxymoronic image reminiscent of the baroque: a chain in echo and implication thus extending from one line to another, and reread also: "sombre . . . eaux / eau sombre; "sombre . . . ô / ô sombre." Lastly in our rereading, one line has been prepared at length in our consciousness by successive texts and strengthened by the hidden verbal weapon (*l'arme*) preceding it and guarding it, resplendent; "Ô lumière et néant de la lumière, ô larmes" sheds now another light on all the texts in their layering: "signe . . . ô sombre." As the dark sign thus founders in the obscure waters, lit only by the double reading of "sombre" as adjective ("somber") and verb ("sombrer" or "sink into"), there returns the memory of the Arthurian sword pulled from the stone of being, in an earlier text marked by its title as one of trial—"L'Ordalie": "Le fer rouge de l'être ne troua plus / La grisaille du verbe . . ." ("The red sword of being no longer pierced / The gray of the word. . . ," *DM,* 179). The gray voice and the gray word are already lost by their lack of color, and are here swallowed up once more irrevocably, like the Arthurian sword, beneath the water itself devoid of color, as the cycle of myth, of legend, and of the poem closes upon itself.

Now the answer to be given to the question "Et toi . . . *qui es-tu?*" might have been "that speech which was silence," as the song fallen silent, *"qui s'est tu,"* is seen in retrospect reflecting back on it in an echo. The sword or the song surfaces once more only through the reading and rereading of this whole volume in its most somber light. When the text itself falls silent, a triple closing-off is felt through these same echoes, as they are prolonged. "Vois, déjà tous chemins que tu suivais se ferment." For with this last voice there fails a vision ("vois"/"see") and also a way of going ("voie"/"path"). Now the real passage will lead from the closure of this path, the failure of this sight, to the eventual opening of an inner threshold, another higher song heard, or understood, within the first song stilled.

Place.   As we have seen, Bonnefoy calls the place of poetry a true one, a *vrai lieu,* a place of sacrifice, no longer a forest opened— as in *Douve* the trees make and then hide the path—but an orangerie closed off and empty of all shadow. The vacant self (this "moi vacant") is determined by its waiting and its watching (like the

surrealist state of readiness, the *état d'attente*), but also by its potential
act, which entails gesture and possession, doubt and risk, speech
and meaning:

> Je ne sais pas si je suis vainqueur. Mais j'ai saisi
> D'un grand coeur l'arme enclose dans la pierre.
> J'ai parlé dans la nuit de l'arme, j'ai risqué
> Le sens et au-delà du sens le monde froid. (*P,* 138)

> (I know not if I am victorious. But I have seized
> Willingly the weapon enclosed in stone.
> I have spoken in the weapon's night, have risked
> Meaning and past meaning the cold world.)

But the gesture of the poet as he grasps the red flame of the sword,
the poetic word held ardent against the grey of a neutral prose is,
to all appearances, a modest one: "Je ne prétends que nommer"
("My only intention is to name," *I,* 25). And Bonnefoy names not
the juxtaposition of two distant elements in the brilliance of a
clashing image, in all the optimism of Breton's surrealist formula
borrowed from Reverdy, nor does he claim that in the world of the
new poetry, words have no more marks on them of the already
decided, and that they have lost the wrinkles of age, both senses of
Breton's essay ("Les mots sans rides"). Nor does it suffice for him
to name, or to see, in order to create: his recognition is just as surely
directed toward what already exists, but is fleeting. The "profound
and paradoxical return towards being" (*I,* 139) of which he speaks
is accomplished only by calling after that which is passing, with
which the poem may primarily concern itself, not to keep it, but
rather to acknowledge its passing. "What does the poem care about,
if it is not to name what is being lost?" (*I,* 139).

For the true place of poetry is also a name, a *vrai nom,* perceived
in the most minimal elements: in one leaf, or in one note of a
birdsong or in one stone only, as the place of an essential return:
"But I come back to the cry of the bird as if to my absolute stone"
(*I,* 37). So that the place of the Arthurian gesture, the tradition of
sword and stone and act, is distinguished quite simply. We are
called and contained by the least of things: "this leaf broken . . .
this leaf . . . this infinite leaf is pure presence," In the tearing of
that leaf lies the profundity of all being. This is the real place of
the world rendered to us through our senses: "Here is the sensible

world . . . here is this sensible world . . . I shall say that it is distant from us like a forbidden city. But I should also say that it is in each one of us like a possible city. Nothing can prevent the soul really attached to it from discovering this threshold and fixing its sojourn there . . ." (*I,* 33). And the way to the sensible world is through the word itself torn and broken like the leaf, just as modest and just as near to hand.

For the name we have only the one we assign, and, as truth, only the name discovered. Language wages war against nothingness, and the word "is the soul of what it names . . . always intact" (*AP,* 185). And yet the search within the sensible for the name in its truth, or the true presence, takes the path not of assurance, but of a doubt, unassuaged even within the place of the word, which we might choose unwisely. The gesture of poetry must therefore be made in the acknowledgment of its uncertainty and of passing. It is against the legendary background of the medieval epic that the poet speaks here, or hesitates: "For one moment everything was lacking. . . ." That the sword is pulled at last from the stone may be no guarantee of the efficacy of the gesture or the durability of the text, but the elements of fire, water, and earth do lend us assurance of the universal. The poet identifies his act with that of a timeless self and with an eternal flowing of the voice of poetry, all the greater for its eventual ceasing.

> Mais enfin le feu se leva,
> Le plus violent navire
> Entra au port.
>
> Aube d'un second jour,
> Je suis enfin venu dans ta maison brûlante
> Et j'ai rompu ce pain où l'eau lointaine coule. (*P,* 138)
>
> (But at last the fire lifted,
> The most violent ship
> Entered the port.
>
> Dawn of a second day,
> I have come at last into your burning house
> And I have broken this bread where the distant water runs.)

Poetry is this risk of sense and dramatic gesture toward meaning, a legendary engraving made in and against the written stone, the *pierre écrite* of the poem: "What is traced in the stone exists, in the most pathetic and strongest sense of that word" (*I,* 18). If the absolute stone is an absolute presence, it is nevertheless a tragic one. What the greatest of our contemporary poets have to offer us is perhaps never anything else but the most anguishing and ardent of melancholies: "That is at least the one gift that a real poet can make. And in his poverty, giving remains his possession" (*AP,* 185). This is at last the true place of the true poet, the essence of his name and of his gift.

Understanding.   In this poetry the absence of all sound, a "noble silence," seems to carry the highest value. As a preliminary stage on the way to reading these texts of a paradoxical silence, the traces and varied inscriptions of the word "understanding" itself may guide us, as they are found in *L'Arrière-Pays.*

We take here the bare structure of certain statements in an effort to perceive their way of presentation. The first moment is an exterior one, and it opens with a question where the doubt is instantly reversed to an answer, positive: "Did I understand. . . ? But we entered into that enclosure and then into the fortress above, and passing through shadowed courtyards and somber rooms we reached terraces where, suddenly, I understood" (*AP,* 52). Here comprehension is seen depending on a deliberately marked passage of entrance, and then on a height sought out as if it might yield an intensity of vision. The architecture of the actual construction, and the verbal structure parallel to it, respond to the search for the understanding of the place.

But subsequently, in a harmonic reprise, this first look is rejected for another, seemingly slower: "No, it is rather that I did not know, in my first look, how to understand everything—which now I do" (*AP,* 54). In the second moment, the look is cast against a screen of a ruined exterior world, bearing the destructive traces of a time gone by, and is gradually transferred toward the interior, toward the unconscious and then understanding of the self as the true place of the human project: "This wall had hidden in its ruin only the unconscious which my visions projected onto it, and which I should first try to understand . . . the temptation had been strong enough, the trial sudden enough, harsh enough, for me to feel in this moment of respite—or to think I felt—that I had the task of understanding myself" (*AP,* 82).

But then again, in a negative replaying of the initial project of comprehension, that hope also is overthrown: "I gave up my ambition to understand, when it was still . . . that which seemed to me the only legitimate intention." Finally, a third act opens with a statement of triumph: "But there was no longer any need to wait for anything at all. I understood, I knew" (*AP,* 123).

Here the poet is finally saved from his private and solipsistic meditation, doomed insofar as it can, by itself, lead nowhere; the mediation of another's sight, for instance, that of a great artist like Poussin, may alter his comprehension. But that realization is at once deeply confident and supremely tragic: for even if we grant that Poussin, chosen by Bonnefoy as the artist seeking the infinite in the finite, and whose work contains the conflicts and the divisions of his private and yet common *Arrière-pays,* is an example of the dilemma's possible resolution, his sight, his understanding, and his decision are still inscribed under his name, and not that of the poet Bonnefoy—unless, like the beauty of a life, the landscape of another can be *assumed,* in the deepest sense.

When the entire journey of and through understanding in all its problematic and sinuous path is redeemed from the destruction of time, like the infant Moses held high above the waters by a girl washing clothes there and whose eyes sparkle like the river, it is both the painter and the poet after him who observe the salvation on which the text closes: "And Poussin, who bears in himself all the tendencies, all the conflicts, for the reconciliations, rediscoveries, miracles even, of a last act of the Universe, of the mind . . . Poussin looks, understands, and decides to paint, master of the golden fleece if there ever was one, his great canvasses of *Moses Saved*" (*AP,* 154–55). So the book too is saved, and the act of painting, and the act of poetry with it. Understanding is the single quality which holds out some possibility of salvation through and to the texts which claim imperfection as their summit, effacement as their greatest clarity, and the final stilling of the voice as their surest interior harmony.

On This Poetry. Finally, a few general comments. I have thought it preferable, as I have pointed out, to speak of each of the volumes in turn, wishing not to confuse any of the written stones with each other. Yet, in order to situate the poems without the distinction from each other which is characteristic more of other poets than of this one, I have chosen not to analyze particular poems but rather to informally describe, even to narrate, the specific, substantial, and nevertheless continuous parts of each volume, hoping to keep the characteristics cumulative, and increasingly clear, before the reader's eyes. By the time the commentary reaches the final volume, *Dans le leurre du seuil,* narration was often seen to give way to more general reflections, such as that on color, specifically, the color red but on color in general, on figures, and on the appearance of the poetry as a whole. The present section will pick up on those remarks and enlarge them: but the reader who might have skipped over the individual descriptions of volumes to arrive at this more general description, would perhaps be well advised to read the generalizing parts of the last section, on which this one builds.

I have tried, for example, to put the reader on guard against the ordinary decoding of colors and qualities as attached to the matter or element to which they seem first to relate: as in some contemporary paintings—and, for instance, in some of Mondrian as early as 1909, and certainly his *Red Cloud,* the title of which Bonnefoy took for a recent book of criticism. As with some of Mondrian's trees of the same period, increasingly up through the year 1913, the nonrepresentative takes on a larger role, just so one should read the color "red," for example, in Bonnefoy. It is not a necessary defining mark of the thing seen, nor is it a symbol, it neither coincides necessarily either with the noun with which presumably it is associated or with any abstract quality, such as sadness or passion: it is not anything, often, other than itself.

It would be ill-considered to dwell on the degree of abstraction in Yves Bonnefoy; I am thinking of his emphasis on the specific as opposed to the concept, of his attachment to the here and the now, and to the minimal object "real," "before our eyes," "on our table," and so on. But it would be equally inadvisable to discount altogether the possible isolation of color from its covering function: it is not, then, exact as a match for a face or dress or body, but significant in itself.

Furthermore, the simplicity of the figures in this poetry is one of the greatest attractions; the images are not filled out in their details, and thus they avoid the platitudes of everyday description. And yet they are sufficiently specific to avoid vagueness, as in the opposing details of the *vanitas* in *L'Anti-Platon.* Specific, yet mysterious, his images are tinged with some odd resonance of an else-where. The affective value of the very few images Bonnefoy uses—ship, salamander, and summer, ivy and foliage, wind and fire, stream, star and threshold—contain all the more remarkable car-rying power for their use and reuse, never appearing arbitrary. They seem necessary and essential, larger than life, minimal and suggestive.

Thus the leaf of ivy as a wonderfully imperfect and even soiled image of possession by the human is opposed to an entire tree or a whole arbor in its greenest green. The imperfection of human words and objects is appealing in itself, and the emphasis on the sparseness of the images and on the elements of narration—some stones and some voices—permits a space to be left around the objects loved and powerful in their attraction. They loom large, but without taking on the abstractness of the concept so abhorred by Bonnefoy. Pathos and joy are gathered about these elements, like concretions of emotion, and in the moment of purest intensity the simplest verse suffices, as for example, the following lines already reappearing: "Ô lumière et néant de la lumière, ô larmes / Souriantes plus haut que l'angoisse ou l'espoir" ("Oh light and nothingness of light, oh tears / Smiling higher than anguish or hope," 137).

The light, simple, neither stating nor representing anything, has more force within it than either human anguish or human hope; it need not be reduced to either or translated into either. A single exclamation, "Oh," suffices to set the noun addressed into relief, eliminating the need for adjectival support. We might compare this technique to the accumulations seen in the final part of the last volume, answered by the reply "Et," the sound, as we have seen, repeated in order to stress the cumulative value of the reply. Or then the initial "oui" of the entire conclusion, stressing the affirm-ative, by particular repetition of the same small monosyllable. The bareness of syntax, the simplicity of the techniques of initial stress, mark the high moments of Bonnefoy's poetry as surely as anaphora marks surrealist poetry: "Breton's "Union libre"—"Ma femme à la . . . Ma femme au . . . Ma femme à la . . ." —or Apollinaire's catalog with "Il y a . . . Il y a . . ." predating Breton's "il y aura une fois. . . ." (See, for instance, Bonnefoy's "Les Guetteurs": "Il y avait un couloir au fond du jardin . . . / Il y avait une étagère dans ma chambre . . . / Il y avait un escalier, et je rêvais . . ." ["There was a corridor at the back of the garden . . . / There were shelves in my room . . . / There was a stair, and I was dream-

ing. . . ," 112]: here the marvelous dream is set off by the un-
spectacular quality of stair, shelves corridor, garden.)

As with the passages beginning by "Et" or "Oui," the repetitive
forms often set the pace, solemn and slow. Such a prose poem as
"Dévotion" with its recurring dedication—"To St.-Yves de la Sa-
gesse . . . To Delphi, where I can live"—is a prime example of
the genre. Let me choose some other texts for illustration, from
different periods and tones. From *Douve:* "Je nommerai désert ce
château que tu fus. . . . / Je nommerai néant l'éclair qui t'a
porté. . . . / Je te nommerai guerre . . ." ("I shall name desert
this castle you were. . . . / I shall name nothing the lightning
flash which bore you. . . . / I shall name you war . . ." (D, 51).
From *Hier régnant désert:*

> L'oiseau qui s'est dépris d'être Phoenix
> ....
> Il sera bien un jour,
> Il saura bien un jour. . . .

> (The bird who was tired of being the Phoenix
> ....
> One day he will be,
> One day he will know how. . . .)

> L'oiseau se défera par misère profonde
> ....
> Il vieillira. . . .
> ....
> Il se taira. . . . Il fera
> Dans l'inutilité d'être les quelques pas
> ....
> Il saura bien mourir. . . . (*HRD,* 101–2)

> (The bird will undo himself in deep misery
> ....
> He will grow old. . . .
> ....
> He will fall silent . . . He will take
> The few steps in the uselessness of being
> ....
> He will know how to die.)

The last few lines I have quoted before, in another context: they refer back, visibly, to the first lines, completing them, repeating them, like the refrain of one of the ancient songs, where the peculiar resonance of the few notes suffices. Here again, it is to be noticed that the *kind* of bird is not named, and that the very namelessness contributes to the isolation and breadth of the figure: the bird singing in medieval times is still now singing.

Many of the most effective of these repetitions are found in *Dans le leurre du seuil,* where they signal the moments of high intensity. The following alternation is carried out over a number of pages without losing its force, rather, gaining momentum and preserving a high pitch: I shall excerpt the stressed repetitions, so as to mark the structure in its extraordinary crescendo:

> Je crie, Regarde
> ....
> Je crie, Regarde
> Ô flamme
> Qui consumant célèbres
>
> ....
> Flamme, oui. . . .
> ....
> Flamme qui vas
> Flamme
> Notre chambre de l'autre année
>
> ....
> Flamme le verre
> ....
> Flamme de salle en salle
> ....
> Flamme l'ampoule
> ....
> Flamme
> Dans la paix de la flamme
> ....
> Je crie, Regarde
> ....
> Je crie, Regarde
> ....
> Je crie, Écoute
> Regarde
> ....

Regarde
. . . .
Je crie, Regarde,
Le signe est devenu le lieu. (*DLS,* 271–78)

(I cry, Look
. . . .
I cry, Look
. . . .
Oh flame
You consume while celebrating
. . . .
Flame, yes. . . .
. . . .
Flame
Our room of the other year
. . . .
Flame the glass
. . . .
Flame, from room to room
. . . .
Flame the lightbulb
Flame
The vine of the flash over there
. . . .
Flame
In the peace of the flame
. . . .
I cry, Look
. . . .
I cry, Look
. . . .
I cry, Listen
. . . .
Look
. . . . .
Look
. . . . .
I cry, Look,
The sign has become the place.)

The reader's look, drawn by the narrator to the text and to the
image, is captured, is directed in turn toward the flame in all its

variants: burning alone, burning in the room from before, burning as the glass, moving from room to room, burning in the light, burning in the vine, until the peace of the flame resumes all the avatars into one full image. Then the cry summoning the sight returns, accompanied by the summons to the ear, returning to the sight, and finally the great statement after the eight-page crescendo, making the résumé of the whole: the *sign alone,* where the word, the color, the figure, is now sufficient unto itself, and no longer needs to represent any other thing or sentiment. The look and the hearing are summoned, in themselves and for themselves. Toward this end, the bare structuring I have tried to show here is the mediation, itself nonrepresentative: We should "look" at the text, and "listen" to it, seeing the seeing and hearing the hearing, not as the sign of something else, but as the place of poetry.

Last, just as inversions are common in Bonnefoy's prose work, giving it a slightly old-fashioned appeal, so in the poetry, interrogations, like the following lengthy one, are spaced between the more direct statements or narrations or descriptions:

> N'avions-nous pas l'été à franchir, comme un large
> Océan immobile, et moi simple, couché
>
> . . . .
> Aimant l'été. . . .
>
> N'étais-je pas le rêve. . . .
> . . . .
> Pour un été plus grand, où rien ne peut finir? (169)
>
> (Did we not have the summer to cross, like a wide
> Motionless ocean, and I, simple, lying down
>
> . . . .
> Loving the summer. . . .
>
> Was I not the dream. . . .
> . . . .
> For a greater summer, where nothing can end?)

The play between the rhetorical question with its inversion and the repetition of the haunting season—the summer loved, in its end-

lessness, in its motionlessness, in its simplicity, and its welcome of
the dream—haunts the text itself.

This passage is taken from the beginning of *Pierre écrite,* where a
balance is established between the slow solemnity of the summer's
presentation and the sudden invocation of the sky as its shoulder
presses against the earth—between those two movements is set this
grave nostalgia of a summertime. The whole illustrates the kind of
sober equilibrium Bonnefoy sets up between the parts of his discourse, which I am illustrating part by part, for the entirety to be
grasped as it is so efficaciously worked out:

> Longtemps ce fut l'été. Une étoile immobile
> Dominait les soleils tournants. L'été de nuit
> Portait l'été de jour dans ses mains de lumière
> Et nous nous parlions bas, en feuillage de nuit.
>
> L'étoile indifférente; et l'étrave; et le clair
> Chemin de l'une à l'autre en eaux et ciels tranquilles. (*PE,* 168)
>
> (For a long time it was summer. An immobile star
> Dominated the spinning suns. The night summer
> Bore the day summer in its hands of light
> And we spoke softly to each other, in night foliage.
>
> The indifferent star; and the stem; and the clear
> Path from one to the other in tranquil waters and skies.)

The text ends with a ship, representing all that is, gliding without
a goal, then the questions initiate the crossing of the summer, as
a ship would cross an ocean, and finally, the invocation to the
shoulder of night, approaching the earth, prepares a welcome: "Ac-
cueille-nous, qui avons goût de fruits qui tombent" ("Welcome us,
who have a taste for falling fruits," 170). Question is placed against
beseeching, dream against fact, stone and voice against voice, all
this seen in the few elements standing out from the rest, which are
to be, like the few words, the salvation of speech and sight and
sign, that is, of poetry.

Overall, Bonnefoy's poetry is one of moderation and control on
the surface, with the sadness at our invincible loss measured against
our moments of joy, to which attention is newly drawn: "Look!"

Anguish at time passing is salved by the hope of an art capable of preserving value, in a few words, like the heavens. The very limited number of images and figures, the very sobriety of presentation, and the balance and equilibrium of tones, suggest to the reader a way of receiving these poems in their symphonic whole.

I would call mine a quiet reading, which in no way should vitiate the gravest and deepest emotions expressed and aroused, but should rather place them behind a screen of simplicity and measure, transparent to the look yet insisting on a tempering of the flame. Thus, I think, the prevalence of mythological situations, the figuration of systems other than the everyday and the present ones. Thus, the Maenads, the Phoenix, the salamander, and even the figure of Douve: these larger-than-life figures set the poetry at a remove, as in a fresco, whose colors are at once bright and dulled, whose lines and spaces do not press indiscreetly upon the perception, but rather invite the gaze and the eventual participation of the reader in the sentiments expressed, with no coercion and no enforced intimacy. At a further risk of an old-fashioned terminology, I would call the texts noble in their restraint, and all the more moving for that, such restraint never to be confused with passivity or with even the neutrality of the classic gaze. The poetry is both focused and of wide reach, noble and simple.

Chapter Three
Watching and Reading
Art and its Essays

In the dedication of Bonnefoy's first volume of essays many of his future themes are announced. It is dedicated to the improbable:

That is to say, to what is.
   To a spirit of watchfulness. To negative theologies. To a poetry desired, of rains, waiting, and wind.
   To a great realism, aggravating instead of resolving, designating the obscure, holding clarities to be clouds easily rent. Caring about a high and impassive clarity. (*I*, 7)

Immediately, the spirit of contradiction is announced. Rather than the possible or the probable, this unlikely state of affairs which is existence attracts attention, as does negative theology in the place of a positive or more ordinary theology. The positive holds out nothing sufficiently ambiguous to involve the poetic spirit. Whereas the statement that what *is* is not what we expect, but its improbable contrary; it arouses the watchful mind responsible for the potentialities of poetry-on-the-wait. Here the heritage from surrealism is clear, and also the extent of Bonnefoy's reaction to it. "The possible," Breton had said, "is what tends to become the real." And he had meant thereby to call attention to the range of what is not yet, to the so-far-unthought, the *impensé* in place of both the *pensé* (what has been thought) and the *pensée* (thought itself).

   Bonnefoy's entire manner is different, and his cast of mind. Nature enters here, as it rarely does in surrealism, except as a metaphor; here the rain and wind are not, in any ordinary sense, metaphoric, but are rather real, forming the surroundings for the expectation, as man is himself placed in the center of his natural environment. As for watchfulness, we remember also from surrealism the privilege of waiting, of the *disponibilité* which was called the truest state of the surrealist, always on the lookout for signs and signals which could then be interpreted as guides for conduct, as the connectors of outside events and inside longing, conscious or unexpected. Bonnefoy assures the attentiveness, but (and again, to our surprise after we have read the first few lines) joins it to a realm in no way simple, an aggravating, disturbing, complicating, *imperfecting* way of seeing. Elsewhere, he will say that "Imperfection is the summit." The unperfecting spirit of the real, now newly defined, opens instead of closing off, makes nothing easy, accepts no facile solutions, is never satisfied with the way things are ordinarily perceived. The high, bright, and impenetrable end of the dedication is placed in a subjunctive framework to indicate the so-far-unlocated state of the clarity sought; and there is no claim made for this realism itself to exist, rather, it *might* exist.

Thus the dedication, and the improbability of its own assumption of the improbable as "existing": the mind at work in the presentation of these essays is never simply concerned with the simple as such and the linear; when there is to be simplicity, even it will be a "second" one. When there is to be an earth, for example, at the center of the essay "Terre seconde," it will be a "second Earth," and so on. If I have entered so unhurriedly into a discussion of the initial lines of this volume, quite unlike the pace followed elsewhere in these pages, it is chiefly because the very notion of such a dedication gives the best idea of the setting appropriate to the thought.

From the "Dédication" to the "Dévotion" which closes the volume, with its echoes and anti-echoes of Rimbaud, *L'Improbable* is presented in a deliberate arrangement like a surrounding frame. The initial essay, "The Tombs of Ravenna," directs toward the monuments of death a positive look, as the next volume, *Un Rêve fait à Mantoue (A Dream in Mantua)* will place its reflections on French poetry in a décor of Byzantine splendor, and will make from ruin, hope. This essay on tombs, published in 1953, marks a definite stage in the maturing of a poetic mind. Among all the essays this one has a particular appeal, a brilliant and yet somber meditation on stones and forgetfulness, on land and country, on life and on death. It is here that Bonnefoy expresses for the first time his thoughts on the concept as a refusal, as an escape from death, on the limited as a "Provisional but sufficient immortality" (*I*, 13).

As often in Bonnefoy's thought, the specific is valued even as it is terrible and melancholy: of the footstep approaching at dark, of a cry or empty house, or the falling of a stone in the shrubbery, there is no concept, but these also make up the real elements of a life, as real as the other, conceptual ones. Like the concept and unlike the specific or the emotional, decoration or an ornament is a "closed world," part of a system, but it joins the universal with the singular: it is the Idea made presence (*I*, 22). Furthermore, the universal must be rethought: it is not abstract, is not the same everywhere, and thus is valid nowhere. And yet, in the specific, strangely, "The universal has its place, in each place, in the gaze directed at it, the use which can be made of it" (*I*, 23). That thought leads directly to the idea of a true place, an idea at the center of Bonnefoy's concern, being the "threshold of the possession of being" (*I*, 23) and thus the place governing the person: "here (the true place is always a here), here reality mute or distant and my existence are met, mutually converted, and mutually exalted in the sufficiency of being" (*I*, 23). The search for this true place lies at the heart of the volume.

This search is not to be separated from the idea of voyage, which is also the idea of poetry. These actions, travel and poetry, alone have some point, says Bonnefoy, and are not divorced from the reality of the sensible; unlike the concept, they can address themselves to questions such as the judgment of beauty and the value of the aesthetic as connected to the moral: "Why are some forms beautiful?" "Why does the sight of stone bring peace to the hearth?" (*I*, 24). Of the sensible world, the signs must be deciphered; Ravenna ("majestic and simple town") exemplifies a silent destiny, a pure utopia, an ethics traversed by the rays of its sun, and still now, "the theater of our potential action" (*I*, 25). If the sensible object is a presence for Bonnefoy, that presence in its act is "the tragedy of the world and its outcome," represented or rather allegorized by one tattered and bruised ivy leaf, green and black. This simple fragment is the contrary of a whole leaf in its immutable essence, that is, of a concept; it summons us and contains us, immortal because, already destroyed, it is thus indestructible in the future.

And such an epiphanic moment as that realization (of the conjunction of our mortality and an immortality sensed) is remembered also in a bird cry, at the top of some cliff, in an instant of perfect solitude. Here we might remember Rilke's meditations at Duino:

He remembered the hour spent in that other garden, in the South: a bird cry was there suddenly, in accord outside and in himself; that is to say, that it was not refracted at the limits of the body, that it reconciled the two directions in an uninterrupted space, where, mysteriously protected, there persisted only a spot of the purest and the deepest consciousness. He had, then, closed his eyes so that such a noble experience was not disturbed by the contours of his body, and the infinite submerged him from all sides with such an intimacy that he believed he could feel in his chest the light weight of the stars which had just risen.

And he explains further, in a letter of 20 February, 1914 to Lou Andréas-Salomé, quoted in the Spender-Leishman translations of the *Duino Elegies,* the exquisite position of the bird, in the path toward the interior":

That is why he sings in the heart of the world as if he were singing in his own interior, and why, also, we take the bird cry so easily for our interior, and feel we translate it, with no reservations, into our own feeling. Yes, this cry can, for one instant, transform the world entirely into interior space, because we feel that the bird does not distinguish between his own heart and that of the world.

What have generalities and concepts to do with the bird song? What matters about the specific image? Later, says Bonnefoy, he was to build on some generalities, but has always returned to the bird cry as to his "absolute stone." Since heaven is not, presence must become our ethics and our freedom, the word to which the highest good is attached: thus the value of poetry.

Baudelaire is, at this point, and remains, with Rimbaud, an important representative for Bonnefoy, of the truth of the word. Even to speak of *Les Fleurs du Mal (The Flowers of Evil)* is to risk betraying it, and falsifying its basic tenets. Baudelaire himself, having suffered, has won the right to be left in peace; having desired the universal, he should be permitted to vanish into it. But also, having been reduced by misunderstanding to the best of himself and the most obscure, he has become our common possession, his life and works serving as examples of the negative theory of which the dedication of this present volume speaks. At the exact summit of violence and unrest, where the contraries wage an unremitting battle, he consents to be himself.

Now his value remains all the more remarkable in that, by its form, *Les Fleurs du mal* seems to belong to the realm of *discourse.* In that realm, logical thoughts, precise statements, and definite descriptions are accustomed to make a conceptual chain, an uncommitting sort of "game" Bonnefoy considers too easy for the speaker, and unrelated to the dangerous commitments of poetry, itself never without risk to the poet. Discourse is related, that is, to the concept, suppresses what is uncertain or excessive, such as the joy and suffering of the thought of nothingness and of death. Baudelaire himself, however, totally unlike his discourse, not only names death but sees it vivid in his own being, making of his own body its tragic theater. "A wounded body and an immortal language" are met for the first time in French poetry, yielding at once clarity and a despairing pain. Baudelaire's gravest disappointment is that the poet is only an actor, dispossessed and hesitant. "He expected strength for death. He obtains only a sullied world" (*I*, 46). The great sacrificial idea is inscribed in poetry as a vision of suffering brought back to life, and poetry is opened by it to the religious spirit. Baudelaire in his affirmation that death can be efficacious, alone able to create once more the lost unity of man, is the ancestor of Mallarmé and Proust, Artaud and Jouve, and also, as it is abundantly clear, although not stated, Yves Bonnefoy.

Oppositions often clarify. Valéry is situated at the opposite pole from Baudelaire and from Bonnefoy, as is immediately obvious: "There was a strength in Valéry but it was lost," begins the chapter devoted to him (*I*, 137). The Mediterranean of the mind, full of the "images of clarity," provides a country where feeling is too easy, where the light never hides anything, nor is it hidden: there, the being swept along by time is not confronted in his real hereness and nowness. Here the peace of language is incapable of action and bare of soul, the word remaining distant from this particular real thing and from the acknowledgment of death. Valéry's project has nothing to do with what Bonnefoy conceives of as the truest role of poetry, which, like love, is to decide what beings are: "It should consecrate itself to this Here and this Now that Hegel had pridefully revoked in the name of language, making of its words which, in fact, desert being, a profound and paradoxical return toward it" (*I*, 139).

The poem should be the meditation of death, before anything else; but Valéry, in Bonnefoy's wonderful expression, "Never found out that death had been invented" (*I*, 140). "His universe holds that our action in it should be unreal. . . . When the only real act is to hurl oneself into what is outside oneself, to approach as nearly as possible a world of our absence, the only act left to Valéry is to retire from every act in order to enrich with a part of divine intelligence our limited condition" (*I,* 140–41). Now the opposition is extreme. It seems to me that the harshest words Bonnefoy finds for any poetry are those devoted to Valéry: even the existence of Monsieur Teste, who has "nothing to say," is a dead gesture, he says, proving only that too much grandeur is granted to the operations of the mind. (Since that remarkable creation of a thinker—modeled on Degas—has had an enormous influence on contemporary thought, as an analogue of "monsieur Text," these comments are instantly and insistently striking.)

By poetics, Valéry tries to submit the poem to science and knowledge, and is thus always prevented from really being a poet by his incapacity to introduce nothingness into the dwelling of essences, as Bonnefoy explains it. "A dandy of the possible" (*I,* 143), he only manages to "sketch out a gesture:" here Bonnefoy may be referring to Valéry's "Ébauches" ("Sketches"). This poetry makes, finally, no place for the specific: for the passerby, as in Baudelaire's great poem on the "Passante," already alluded to in this commentary. No room for a particular swan—here we think of Mallarmé's great sonnet on the swan frozen in the lake, a sonnet on death and poetry—or even for a torn and bruised ivy leaf marked with mud, able to signify and make present the real. Since he does not love things, Bonnefoy concludes, Valéry is, rather than Baudelaire or the others to whom the title might have been thought to apply more readily, the true condemned man, the *maudit* of French poetry.

The essay closes on an unforgettable note: the "Cimetière marin," the "Cemetery by the Sea," is Valéry's most beautiful poem, claims Bonnefoy, "because there he hesitates." But unfortunately again, Valéry seems to prefer a sort of "colorless sadness" to an anguish that would have been creative. His art is an art of closed form, which rejects for example the mute *e,* the one *fault* characteristic of French poetry, and then identifies form with the conscious mind, with the daylight, rejecting all rupture and night and imperfection, rejecting, that is, the real. "We must forget Valéry," says Bonnefoy, and yet his single footnote here, the only one in all these essays, gives a visible clue to the importance of his commentary. I shall quote the footnote in entirety:

Did I criticize Valéry? I took him seriously, I think, an honor one can
bestow on a very small number of writers. And those continue to exist *in
us*. We must struggle against them, as we must choose, and in order to
be. This is a private struggle. Perhaps it is a bet, in the slightly grave
sense which can be given to this word. (*I,* 146)

In his essays on artists, Bonnefoy is particularly given to comparisons
and contrasts, revealing a vivacity of perception which, like all good
commentaries on art, enables the reader to see afresh. As with the
Valéry/Baudelaire opposition, these pairings clarify. Bonnefoy compares, for example, a painting of Balthus with the light in Piero
della Francesca, and the reader finds no difficulty in perceiving in
parallel a painting of the Italian fifteenth century and of a French
twentieth-century artist: "Finally, movement and life have been
chased from the center of being. The leaden skies of this frightening
evening are the successors to Piero's eternal noon" (*I,* 73). Or again
a contrast: as the duality of Balthus's work and his ambiguity are
a major part of his attraction for Bonnefoy, the prudent gravity,
the sobriety and exactitude are the major appeal of Ubac: "French
art is never anything else than limitation," says Bonnefoy. Akin
neither to the high noon of Piero nor to the evening of Balthus,
this art is either clear or obscure depending on our own gaze. And
here again, as always, Bonnefoy compares painting to being, stone
to substance, spirit to heart. What is seen is not dissociated from
what is felt, unlike the state of affairs often prevailing in contemporary criticism. The "improbable gift of the instant" is responsible
for the revelations of all artists who pose a problem for us: our self-
consciousness must at once be abolished for us to see, and yet it
must be kept for us to possess the object seen.

Here I return for a moment, as Bonnefoy often does, to the
example of Piero della Francesca: in "Time and the Timeless in
Fifteenth Century Painting" Bonnefoy explains the perceiving-time
involved in our reading of signs in that artist (from blue to the idea
of a cloak, to the Madonna, to her smile, and so on). Again a
contrast is established: Uccello's *Profanation of the Host* is anguished
by a "tragic virtuality" because he loved time; the Magdalene's
candle flame in de La Tour's pictures of her with her Vigil-Lamp
tells its own duration, and its slow and pitiless consumption, and
also the instant of reflection. But time here, and in the Italy of the
Renaissance, is face to face with eternity. Some artists will try to

save the timeless and others will choose to love time itself and for itself; the two schools take cognizance of their opposed attitudes through the idea of perspective, which envisages the invisible as reality. That thought is undone by the necessity of thinking space, of deforming things, and of conceptual speculation, of an hypothesis to be confirmed. The work in perspective supposes a central spectator around whom all is organized, an optimistic project both intellectual and moral, intended to express the soul of what is and as it is, its "number" in the Pythagorean sense. Thus a metaphysical decision is made for a subjective art, which Brunelleschi introduces. But in Piero, human time disappears. The human look is lost, the instant is not understood, death is blotted out. At the conclusion of the essay, poetry is redefined, and the project of what is, after all, our main concern as Bonnefoy presents it, returns. To forget or not to forget death is perhaps the same thing for this matter of seeing and expressing and revealing: with that the artists help us, and for that our perception must be sharpened: to the latter end all the essays in the volume contribute.

The final long essay in the volume is also the major response to the initial essay on tombs, and to the question we may well ask of each poet: what is poetry for you? The conditional identification, made at the outset, between poetry and hope ("I would like to join, would like to make almost identical, poetry and hope") is to be arrived at only after a meditation on refusal, on the word as "the soul of what it names" and the manner in which it designates time and space, as they have dispossessed us. The word, the name, retain the essence of the thing: Dante names Beatrice *because* he has lost her. But we, who do not live among the Gods, who cannot believe in poetic transmutation, have to ask the questions which are hardest: losing, do we close ourselves off in some ivory tower of words, so as not to be hurt by loss? Or cling to the resurrection of that lost object or person among us, at whatever price? In some sense, the answer to this question defines the poet's attitude, in an unforgettable way: Mallarmé would have chosen dispossession in order to save the self from nothingness, or at least chose that attempt, whatever failure his infinite honesty finally acknowledged: "Mallarmé no longer wants to save more than the almond of being, but, because the word seems to be one with it, truly thinks he can. . . . Poetry must save being, which will save us afterwards" (*I*, 152). Bonnefoy will return to a longer and infinitely perceptive treatment of Mallarmé in the superb essay on his poetics used as the preface to the collection of Mallarmé's prose published by Gallimard in the collection *Poésie,* and also in *Le Nuage rouge,* but here in this preliminary discussion of that poet, we read the brief, ironic, and yet moving statement which by itself forms a paragraph: "For Mallarmé arrived only at truth."

Having wanted salvation, language, and truth, that is, he managed to attain only the latter, for our syntax, no matter how it is altered, elliptical, transfigured, transformed, and deformed, is only "a metaphor of impossible syntax, signifying only exile" (*I,* 153). The Idea cannot appear in it, but only our distance from facility on the one hand and meaningful reality on the other. For there, the ancient baptismal idea of dying to this world in order to be born again forms the basis of Mallarmé's attitude: "Happily," he writes, "I am completely dead." The appeal and even the fascination of death, the ceremonies and rituals of the obscure, the profound pleasures of refusal, the opposition of the word to the real in Mallarmé— and also Racine—are resumed perfectly in the metaphor of the closed orangerie which Bonnefoy considers the emblem and the latent consciousness of this age. Have no dark parts, being open to the sun on all sides, but with a slight taste of blood, the place of some anterior act and the dwelling of a *moi vacant,* or a self emptied of substance, this orangerie of the essential has an almost obsessive hold on the poetry coming after it.

The essential strictness, the severity and almost the poverty of the consciousness thus simplified characterize Baudelaire as they do Racine. The poetry of the here and now, the limits of love for a specific being and thing, and the passion for words which nevertheless cannot persuade us that they are the real salvation, these cannot take us past what is mortal, cannot guarantee us against death, which is, then, a deep aspect of the presence of beings and in a sense, their only reality. In his breaking of formal perfection, his destruction of beauty, and his choice of death, Baudelaire's desperate consciousness and his strange concomitant joy find the good in the mortal object, like a New Sun, and our salvation in our very mortality. Rimbaud his inheritor reinforces the understanding of poetry as a means, and not an end, of an essential and almost impossible exigency, quite unlike our contemporary poetry of skepticism and withdrawal into scientific "disciplines."

Hope must be reinvented, in spite of our recognition of the truth of such a landscape as Eliot's "Waste Land" of the real, and the love of mortal things reintroduced, after Baudelaire: "Let us stand again on the threshold he thought closed off, before the most depressing proofs of night. . . . Something possible appears upon the ruins of all possibility. . . ." Even if words betray us, "Everything we have lost, formerly, immobile and smiling at doors of light, is returned to us. Everything that passes and does not cease to pass suspends its step which is night . . ." (*I*, 172–73). An event takes place and, as in Rilke, a bird song marks this epiphanic consciousness. Even should we be once again lost in the moment, exiled in time and space, in an opportunity forever missed, we have hope, a limited certainty and the possibility, the duty even, of summoning the real, like Heidegger's own call to disclose or unveil being.

The true place is, as always, that of the here and now. The act of presence and of their presence is the most real and deepest act of poetry; the difficulty will not be eliminated, nor will the incessant struggle in the theater of being and essence. As words are an act, as at least the hypothesis of meaning is our deepest need in order to organize our knowledge, this poetry is anguish and a "negative theology . . . the only universality I recognize in poetry" (*I*, 177–78). The truth of the word and its intuition and expectancy are the act of absolute presence and our real present, our "trial by fire" in its most intense realization: "The true place is a fragment of duration consumed by the eternal: in the true place time is undone in us" (*I*, 181). It is given by chance, but that very chance enables the universe around us to become a place of signs, a dwelling for hope: "And I say that the anguish of the true place is the oath of poetry. Having provided the energy for starting out, it is also the resource of the path. . . . Poetry is carried on in the space of speech, but each step of it is verifiable within the world reaffirmed" (*I*, 182–84).

An "initiatory realism," Bonnefoy suggests, prepares us for this sort of mental motion, attached as it is both to the real and to the hope of something as yet inexpressible. This poetry, while we meditate upon and within it, will not have prevented our aging, will not have suppressed—nor would we choose it to—the myriad contradictions of our exile, or attained any sunlit orangerie of perfect and certain substance and form: "Modern poetry is far from its possible dwelling. The great room with four windows is refused it still. The repose of form in the poem is not honestly acceptable" (*I*, 185). But the luck of poetry to come is worth awaiting, in all the anguish that entails, and is in any case our only possible chance, given what we know and have passed through: "What will we have had, in truth, if we do not attain the true place?" (*I*, 184).

I would say, in conclusion, that the true place for Bonnefoy and, by extension, for his readers, is not only the one made up of the here and now, is not even only some windowpane shining in the evening light on the side of some mountain—that superb and simple image on which the chapter closes—but it is also a waiting and a confidence in the chance of poetry. And in view of that conclusion, the brief and moving "Devotion" at the end of the volume, that eloquent response to Rimbaud, may be reread in the shadow and the light of Ravenna's tombs: the stones are Ravenna's, and all the marks of ruin and death and limitation reappear in these "poorly lit trains" of each evening and the "snowy street under the limitless stars," all of these making their own rediscovery of the here and now, through various manifestations of physical and mental transport: "I was going, I was losing my way. And words were finding their way with difficulty in the terrible silence" (*I*, 189). Words are both patient and saving.

And here, even the most unexceptional rooms ("ces deux salles quelconques") can retain the gods among us. We may not be any longer numbered among them, not sharing their absolute immortality—may not have kept even the same definition of them, and may yet be struggling in our consciousness with them, but our words are part of a voice "consumed by an essential fever," and are to be counted among the real manifestations of our poetic presence.

Un rêve fait à Mantoue (*A Dream in Mantua,* 1967) is inscribed, already by its title, under the double sign of the interior and the exterior: dream and place. Once in Mantua, Bonnefoy took a photograph of Sylvia Beach, and meditates in the title essay upon the relation of such a silent epiphany to the changing light, and upon the desire of humans for an inner, unchanging being. So the individual essays, not all of which I shall comment upon here, might each be seen as parts of this struggle to maintain the interior with a reflection on the exterior, to aim toward essence without letting the aspect disappear from view, to include the lesson of and the visual richness of the dream in that reality which the poem, and the essay, will finally turn out to incorporate.

The threshold essay of the volume, on Byzantium, speaks precisely of the threshold and gives to the volume its orientation. As with many of Bonnefoy's writings, the main focus is placed on the search for a *place*, one that will be central for the heart. "And in this picture I am attempting to make—that of a true country—I want the characteristics of a threshold to be recognizable" (*URM,* 11). Over this threshold we are to make our entry into this other land, where we may flourish in our very individuality and its enforced limits— for death is always present in the thought of Bonnefoy. Yeats, whose poetry Bonnefoy has translated, particularly the great "Sailing to Byzantium" (on the difficulties of which he has written an illuminating essay), puts the accent on an opposition between an automaton, a bejeweled and golden bird, and a real and ephemeral bird: for him, Byzantium is a faraway and eternal refuge of art and culture. Yet Bonnefoy sees in Byzantium not pride and triumph, but the opposite, "no longer Theodora in her gold, but Mitra in ruins, no longer the peacock but the stone—and I have immediately associated it with a desire in me seeking a country, confronting the real in its most fugitive aspects, apparently those the least weighted with being, to consecrate them and for me to be saved with them" (*URM,* 10).

That Byzantium can be—is—both things for these poets so different is part of its appeal, for them and for us, illustrating the multiplication of meanings around one sign. For Bonnefoy, its teaching about limits and about morality makes of it that representation of true place which lets him mark the contrast with Venice, for instance, in its illusion of triumph, or with Rubens, in his. Later, in the long reworking of the essay on Baudelaire and Rubens, the point is still clearer: in the former's intimations of death and of the passing moment (as in Baudelaire's sonnet "To a Passerby") and in the display Rubens makes of the glories of this life, visible in his canvasses. Finitude and the presence it reveals, this great theme of Bonnefoy's work, is illustrated both magnificently and modestly in Byzantium, where eternity is seen not as the negation of the temporal but as its transfiguration and true meaning.

If Bonnefoy chooses the figure of Christ at Sopocani, it is for his transfiguration of the person and the real without the sacrifice of human possibilities, without "changing into fault his finitude,"

without making of suffering an end in itself. This Christ, says
Bonnefoy, seems our most intimate future, able to be interiorized,
and near to present-day poetry. Byzantine art speaks in the name
of the individual and his singular condition, however anxious or
immanent is his return "to the dwelling of being" (URM, 13).
Subjective, and speaking to the being in dispersion, this art differs
from Greek art in not seeking perfect relations between form and
matter, but rather a relation between soul and self. In this refusal
of the perfect also, we recognize one of Bonnefoy's most typical
stances, opposing the perfection of form and preferring its imperfection, for instance, in the mute e of French poetry, this fault made
feeling. For the human and the mortal, those limits accepted (and
not in any sense like the proud enigma of André Breton's statement
about the surrealist "accepting the unacceptable human condition")
are the basis both for poetry and for that true country of which
Byzantium gives the model, and to which it gives a place.

The following essay, "On Painting and Place," reaffirms the
relation between grouped works in manuscript and their surroundings, however arbitrary. One becomes attached to places when the
works found in them matter. Some special light of the atmosphere
may bring clarity to a painting hung in the obscurity of a room,
or the darkness of a room may contribute to a painted shadow, so
that their interrelations matter also. And then too, an arbitrary
surprise can contribute to the joy of perception, such as a completely
unexpected location, where the juncture of the art work and the
place is at best tenuous: a Veronese found in London instead of
Italy, a Botticelli in the redbrick and white painted wood columns
of a New England town, some work of Piero della Francesca in a
"marble mausoleum, somewhere between Massachusetts and Ver-
mont." (Italian art is abundant in ambiguity, both in its substance
and in its odd situations or locations: thus these examples.)

Painting, however, has as its inescapable task the relating of the
objective absolute and the subjective world. Is it not a question of

this *multiple* so fiercely contested by all the arts given over to the Intelligible, affirming itself before them: opposing, to their uncertain hypothesis of the One, the reality of chance in its faultless evidence, so creating,
between the work and its dwelling of exile, a tension which will aggravate
our consciousness of being? Perhaps the only true liturgy of which our

epoch is capable is that of confronting, in order to revitalize them each by the other, the two poles of intuition. (*URM,* 20)

This struggle represents, between the absolute and the individual, the summit of consciousness—but also, of *chance,* which will one day become the roll of dice, says Bonnefoy in response to Mallarmé's debate about the role of chance in *Igitur* and *Un Coup de dés,* and reversing the elements. So, for instance, a copy of a copy, impregnated by a whole tradition of representation, can approach nearer to the center of what matters in art than a completely conscious work of a master. Chance, place, situation: all these count in the ideal reading and understanding of the work of art.

One of these essays, "A Second Simplicity," concerns the baroque, to which another essay here is devoted, as well as the entire volume *Rome 1630.* One might at first be surprised—either because of the title or because of Bonnefoy's own attitude toward the simple as opposed to the ornate—at his choice of the baroque as a subject of interest and even of passion. Without delay, he states the primary reason for his attachment to baroque extravagance: "I love it, even in its bad taste, because I understand it as a heroism, as the reaffirmation of the sensible object in the very heart (how vibrant it is!) of the will of forms. . . . The baroque is a passionate realism . . . loving what passes, it has its limits, and dies . . ." (*URM,* 25). It is above all through the feverish and garish, against all reason, that existence on this earth may participate in divine right, and this art of the baroque came to life just at the time when the elements of religious ritual, the bread and the wine, were no longer understood as the redemption of things, including our place and moment and situation. But above all, in the baroque, Bonnefoy chooses the moment when the concern with ornament and the conflict of forms and number seem to cease, in favor of what Kierkegaard has called "repetition" and Bonnefoy in turn a "second simplicity," a possible approach to an impossible unity. In this second simplicity, the precarious and the temporal are infused with the immobile Law and the Idea, and presence contains the thought of the intemporal. So that the contraries meet and consent, each to the other. "Here the trembling gesture of what is living" (*URM,* 27) takes on the sense of an eternally valuable statement of human effort: the word *tremble* reminds us of the final paragraph of André Malraux's great volume on art, *Les Voix du Silence (The Voices of Silence),* about Rembrandt's gesture made, with a trembling wrist, in the face of stars and civilizations, this challenge of the artist who traces what is highest and yet weak with human weakness:

In that house of shadows where Rembrandt still plies his brush, all the illustrious shades from the artists of the caverns onward, follow each movement of the trembling hand that is drafting for them a new lease of survival—or of sleep.
And that hand whose waverings in the room are watched by ages immemorial is vibrant with one of the loftiest of the secret yet compelling testimonies to the power and the glory of being Man.

Here we become aware of a melancholy, both "healed and not healed," and this, like the nostalgia for the garden, or that privileged or closed-off place of poetry, is not to be shaken off, and penetrates a good deal of Bonnefoy's work: "No, we have not been cured of the garden."

Many of the artists about whom he speaks can be characterized by their strong sense of that kind of nostalgia. Giorgio de Chirico furnishes perhaps the best example of an attempt at rendering the Platonic enterprise, in its double "concern for essence and appearance," and then the closing off of its path. De Chirico does not finally attempt a metaphysical solution, but only pictures a here and now in the apparent triviality of their immediate effect. In his one hanging glove, in his mannequin, in his one artichoke or banana, "the reflection of the rows of arcades is effaced" (URM, 37). The presence and everydayness of being is forbidden the coherence of the abstract, of numbers, as opposed to the ontological imperfection of man. The cast shadows—to which an entire chapter is devoted later in this essay—reveal chance, irreducible as it is, and the finitude of such a place at such a moment. The Intelligible withdraws from the world ineluctably, and from the project capturing it in an architecture of harmonious proportions: "All De Chirico's art is this passage from the interiority of an old project to the meditative contemplation of its wreckage, and of the ambiguous categories which will have stifled it, while permitting it . . ." (URM, 35).

This melancholy and this joy in ambiguity produce a series of essays which haunt the reader in much the same way as de Chirico's canvasses themselves:

Six o'clock in the afternoon toward the end of summer, an empty room, the music of Cimarosa, the thought of people eating ice cream elsewhere under the arcades, the "black sun" of Gérard de Nerval, above all, the "almost absolute" moment in Mozart's *Don Juan,* when the masked figures advance on the dark threshold of the festival: *O belle maschere, cosa chiedete?*

This art—and the essay on "Humor, the Cast Shadows," closes thus—is not directed at the construction of being, but at that of existence and fate. Plainly, this deeply felt ambiguity tinged with sorrow at the irreversibility of all our projects resides at the other pole from the humor of the Piero della Francesca's hats with which the essay began. This deepening of the mental gaze from the exterior detail to the interior meditation, is characteristic of Bonnefoy; the technique serves to project into his essays a deeper meaning.

A series of images from the other essays, not discussed here, remains with us: the figure of Gaston Louis Roux perceived in a garden, of brightness and dark ("A Vine Moving in the Shadows"), Ubac showing his work being stretched out on the ground, the work revealing that "infinite interior" of which Bonnefoy speaks, filled with it, like vases holding a fresh serenity. Elsewhere, a figure of Venus at Paestum holds something buried and yet future, and elsewhere still a house with its walls inscribed by peasants bringing wheat, all these sights are united by a brush stroke of the painter ("Nearness of the Face"). Or again, in "Giacometti's Stranger," the flowers tossed on the open earth at his burial, the mountains cutting the air like knives, or his incessant wandering at nightfall make unforgettable pictures, alongside those of the grey church of Saint-Étienne in Tours covered in rose stone, or some trains at evening, a wounded bird in Ravenna, and a black morning of heavy rain in Seville. Bonnefoy's intensely visual imagination serves him well, as it does his reader. The images together may converge, as in the final pages of the "Seven Fires," in an unconscious richly endowed with figures which could have been joined together; the choice reveals a joyous approach to being, to the real, as the figures join in an interior unity. The event recounted in the chapel at Seville is an interior event, bringing a revelation that will last. Conscious of the multitude of signs on that rainy day in Seville, of the sudden animation in a church of an altar piece and of its meaning—that no one will have to grow old alone and deprived—meditating on his own unconscious and on chance and openness to it as the key to revelation, the poet as person, as dreamer and as critic, sees a shadow flowing around him: "A water, indeed, made of these images and of these breaks in the image, a water of invisibility which dissolves the illusion of forms, nevertheless reborn, which resolves the mortal gaze, a water that we might find at the extreme limit of our attention to works . . ." (URM, 200).

In the memory of a ship sailing to South America, from which children are seen playing and where a great calm is sensed: "I measure space, the relation of shadows to the facades, the trembling of a darkness in the dawn's transparency" (URM, 202). The vision on which the volume closes is to be joined with that of Bonnefoy's tales in L'Ordalie (The Trial) and those of the Rue Traversière (Short-cut Street), but also it makes a perfect end for this present collection of essays, infused as they are with an unquestioned passion, illumined by his introduction of the themes of temporality, at the very moment of comprehension and epiphanic consciousness: "We look and are looked at, all is perfectly calm in the laughing light; but the boat glides on, we are just passing" (URM, 202). This text was published in L'Éphémère (The Ephemeral) where much of Bonnefoy's work first appeared; that the journal itself was planned as and proved to be ephemeral is itself significant in the theme of voyage and its relation to art.

To end such a powerful collection of essays on a theme of passing would be effective alone; but it is all the more effective for its combination with the final paragraph, a dedication to Bernini, the sculptor of a mortuary monument. The essays—one of which remains still to be discussed—are both monumental and deliberately ephemeral, marked by separate occasions: the publication of a book (a French translation of Chestov, or Charpentrat's book on the baroque), by the death of an artist or friend (Jacques Villon, Giacometti, or Sylvia Beach) whose circumstantial and individual trace they frankly bear.

Now I have left for last the major essay of this volume, "French Poetry and the Principle of Identity," which deals with language and poetic intuition, with the special genius of the French tongue, and with the hope for poetry seen from that angle. The simplest apparent difference, say for instance that between a horse and the horse, a fire and the fire, lead Bonnefoy to an essential meditation in which a salamander or then the salamander is the central figure. Appearing suddenly in the fire, he can be ranged in the category of salamanders, one among the others, or then can be questioned as to what he is, and why, and from where he came? The world, quiet in its "evil" or unspeaking presence, gives no answers to this sort of question, and the questioner is absorbed by the idea of death. Or again, as the third possible reaction, the salamander can be lived as an experience, can becomes (or become once more) *the salamander,* in whose pure act of existing, essence is understood. Then the observer is awakened and aroused to his or her deepest being, and all the salamander has touched is consecrated in terms of the new understanding: "The wall is justified, and the hearth: and the olive tree outside, and the earth . . . I have gone from doomed perception to love, the prescience of the invisible" (*URM,* 97).

This invisible is the real, for it alone is left when all particular and visible aspects have dissolved "to leave only a face unseen, the angel or the One of the Eternal instant, when everything is given to me for me to understand and link together" (*URM,* 98). This reestablished unity is called presence; in it the salamander "is" among other presences. Understanding is the opposite of the analysis which dissociates, permits the specificity and the individuality of words to freeze into concepts, leading to the kind of bad silence which is the equivalent of the bad presence already mentioned in these pages. Language, on the other hand, is a structure, and as such can promise beyond its conceptual aspects the same unity as being.

Words, some few words, contain the hope of poetic consciousness for real presence, beyond the aspect and toward the essence. As the English language is richest in the notation of the human gesture and the aspects of things, the richness of the language must be saved: in Shakespeare, image must cancel out image for the invisible to be felt, whereas in French words seem already to contain entities. The best analogy for French poetry, says Bonnefoy, is back-lighting, the *contre-jour;* this sort of light is found in the darkest poem, and some hope of spiritual dawn, in the "other and warmest back-lighting of evening." Bonnefoy's own attitude is always close to the language of indirection, always conscious of the value of difficulty, so that in his approach this back-lighting replaces what some would choose as the full light of noon. Just so, Bonnefoy warns against the facility of naming: for example, to name a tree too easily is to remain a captive of just a poor image of it. The tree is, in any case, an abstract one, which "can only grow in the space of the absolute from one of the aspects, the only one retained of the object—by pure absent-mindedness" (*URM*, 124).

In any language, an order is established, and with it, meaning. The poem has as its aim, not the elaboration of aesthetics, or even an object with a varied structure of meanings, but rather salvation: this is its intention. As the effort to interiorize the real, it joins and connects all things *within the self;* the invisible is not the disappearance of what is seen, but the liberation from it, and so the poem, its preface and its realization, is situated at the highest point of mental being, where it joins outer with inner, space with structure, to order a life and a way of seeing. The salamander, this recurrent figure in Bonnefoy's work, represents and resumes all of that meditation, balanced by the Phoenix, who can be seen to play the same role for the other major themes of his poetry, the other ways of poetic salvation.

Bonnefoy's work, called *Rome 1630: L'horizon du premier baroque* (Rome 1630: The Horizon of the First Baroque, 1970), has a special situation within his writing: in no other epoch does he study so carefully the metaphysical and psychological reasons of the art and its relation to us. The baroque is a movement of conscience, a freedom of choice; the two figures Bonnefoy treats in particular are Bernini and Poussin, the representatives of two different attitudes, in the appositional method characteristic of his approach. (I am thinking, again, of his Baudelaire against Rubens, his Lear against Hamlet, and so on.)

Bernini is discussed as the destroyer of all the claims of the "aspect," that general category invented by the Renaissance and against which the tendency to the specific must wage a determined battle in favor of the *hic* and the *nunc*. Of these latter categories, Bonnefoy believes that Bernini discovered the secret, "of experience, of redemption reserved here and now to the person, absolute, unique . . ." (*R*, 18). Bernini fights also against the attraction of what merely presents itself as a facade: the closed world of appearances "has become once more just seeming . . ." (*R*, 17). What Bernini considers is not the object in itself and its outward presentation, but our relation to it, the "figure of an encounter," as he puts it. The artist operates the transposition of the visual to the existential, the known to the lived. This emphasis on living, on the present, on the here and now is seldom absent from Bonnefoy's greatest moments of passion and reassurance.

Second, Poussin causes a revolution in the way of seeing, for his time and ours: "*True* form, in the perspective taken here, is no longer the exterior form of the object, but the wholly mental one which is established between relations of numbers and colors, in that there is a sort of passage from old geometry to algebra, and from Pythagoras to Descartes, except that the goal is not knowledge. . . ." Perhaps there will be in this most complex world of modern painting, a path leading also from dream to dreamed, where the question of love as the baroque asks it will be reformed little by little starting from its primordial givens: childhood, the true place, woman as redeemer, destiny. Is this not the secret of *Moses Saved from the Waters?* (*R,* 126). On this same canvas the great autobiographical work called *L'Arrière-pays* (The country beyond) will close. In all our contact with being, we need specific persons as mediators, as, in our contact with the visual world, we need specific works of art. The lesson taught here is the same as that reiterated in many forms and places: the now and the here and the single being count above all else. Discovering this, we discover the essential of ancient Rome, which is love.

This conclusion is anything but banal, even if it may seem simple; the baroque as twisted energy, as human strength, as violent contrast: to all of that we are accustomed. But Bonnefoy's suggestion, unfailingly exact, reveals also his own attachment to art and to the human: "Love is to be reinvented," begins his essay on Rimbaud. Not just an exchange of word and world, that "reciprocity of proofs" with which he connects Mallarmé, in his dream of a world both spoken and lived, but also emotion characteristic of the tone and substance of Bonnefoy's own writing, and of the epochs he chooses to dwell upon.

Rome, 1630: the place is clear, and the time: *Hic et nunc.* And perhaps and paradoxically exactly for that reason, his perspective may prove to be a lasting one.

Subtitled "Essays on Poetics," *Le Nuage rouge* (The red cloud) includes all of Bonnefoy's major essays since *Un Rêve fait à Mantoue* and *L'Arrière-pays.* As before, I shall speak only of the principal themes, and shall pass lightly over some essays which are extensions and rethinkings of essays already discussed ("Baudelaire against Rubens," "The Poetics of Mallarmé"). The essays are arranged from the initial and long confrontation of one poet and one painter, which occupies a section by itself, then a section on artists and critics (Bellini, Elsheimer, Morandi, Mondrian, and Duthuit), a section on poets and poetry ("The Song of Roland," Mallarmé, Rimbaud, Perse, and Jouve), and finally a section, responding to the initial juxtaposition, in which creators of the visual (Garache) and of the verbal (Heinein, Celan) make way for the essays on the double phenomenon which closes the volume.

The whole enterprise is inscribed under the image of a red cloud, that of Mondrian, and ends with the cloud as the sign of the simple, as the image under which the words of the Buddhist Bashô are inscribed. Elsewhere, in the long poem "Dans le leurre du seuil" (In the lure of the threshold) the cloud leads the ship; like the salamander, it is a constant index of the relation to the universe as a sign of hope, and joins the separate works each to the other. Under this sign then, the volume sets forth.

The opening frame of the work sets up Rubens against Delacroix and Baudelaire, Rubens as banal or Rubens as melodramatic, mindless, imitative rather than self-determined, or as vulgar, opposed to the "impassioned but cautious work of Delacroix. . . ," for example. Baudelaire sees in Delacroix an artist "miraculous," "profound, mysterious, sensual, terrible" (NR, 62):

a witness to presence but cast into exile by his mysterious impatience from his importunate desire, the painter Delacroix has only his tomb to dig, the painting, this desperate need; but like Baudelaire at Namur, it is really an insistence that the God who is soon to be born from so much passion consummated be there already, to bring him back to life. (NR, 63)

To be a painter entails impossible questions about appearance: should we, or should we not denounce its scandal? Baudelaire the poet will be the "sorrowing hero of this negative theology" (NR, 63), preparing others for such Incarnation as will now take place.

But did not Baudelaire himself substitute appearance for presence, claims Bonnefoy, trying to reconcile the dream with the real, to identify poetry with ambiguity? So Rubens becomes the "strength and the impulse, the fire against which Baudelaire's distress stands out etched in black" (NR, 57). Baudelaire never ceases to doubt, and to lament the treason of the image; but Bonnefoy, who has listened to Baudelaire, who has "followed him in the contradictions of his clairvoyance," yet cannot "fail to oppose to his pessimism a sort of confidence, of which he himself is one of the causes. What a light there is, in fact, in *Les Fleurs du Mal*" (*NR*, 67). And the whole meditation has turned toward the positive: "Before, I could have asked, like Baudelaire, like Pascal, that one choose between writing and presence, vertigo and life, that one choose, even if, concerning my own destiny, I would not accept to do so. But now . . ." (*NR*, 70).

Now there appears a new way of seeing things: presence is, as the baroque writers saw, "That which one decides on . . . it is a dream, of course, made of all the weight of our universe of matter; but if one rises to approach, it will itself rise and come toward us" (*NR*, 72). With the negative theologies of which he has already spoken, there is now mingled a light "from below, from above, from all sides . . . as when an evening sun, returning, is caught in the rain about to cease—a red cloud above the roads" (*NR*, 73). And the poet thinks that this light in which two principles are joined is the path to take, that this writing and this dark fire, as in Poussin's painting of *Moses Saved* to which he often refers, contain the God to be born "who is no one, and will be nothing, shining, however, there on the transfigured roof of some stable, here in some words redeemed" (*NR*, 73). The major sign will come, and will be born into common speech by the confidence of a poet, shared with his readers.

To write, of course—who could ever not have done so? But also to *unwrite*, by an experience complementary to the poem, by the maturing that it alone permits, all the phantasms and chimeras with which our past would otherwise obscure our sight. . . . No, this book that I am finishing is nothing, and precisely because it is everything. The world which seizes upon my sight at this moment of my advance is also the step left behind, the halt made; here progress can start our decision over from some other source; the path, from then on, goes toward this invisible ahead-of-us—which is the place. (*NR*, 76).

As Baudelaire chooses in Rubens what paintings to see, we in return choose passages in Baudelaire. Both retain an ambivalent stance between the here and the now on one hand, the moment and the form of the work on the other. (By contrast, we might think again of Mallarmé, cutting off from all desires of the earthly life of flesh and substance, in favor of form.) For those who wish to reduce the work to only a "text," Bonnefoy reserves his harshest opinion: "Now by gathering that nocturnal honey, we shall lose a land" (*NR*, 80). Between poets and attitudes, a selection must be made: "*Choice*, as such, wanting this or that, putting one's confidence in 'drawing' or then one's value in revolt, being Baudelaire or Rubens, or even Mallarmé, this is the place of poetry" (*NR*, 80).

Of Bellini, that "great painter lost between two ages of the world" (*NR*, 94), of Elsheimer, who rediscovers in his *Derision of Ceres* a lizard appearing briefly as the image of absence, shining and cold, and of Duthuit and his utopia, his "retreat, his inclination to solitude" (*NR*, 166), Bonnefoy writes at some length, and also of Morandi, whose bottles and boxes denounce the superficiality of our language, by creating an irreparable silence, and show the outside of things as it is touched with the "politeness of despair." The conclusion of that essay brings a moral lesson for all of us:

But who will reproach him for having lived so intensely the closing in upon oneself and the fear? To look with an unblinking eye at the lamp, the carafe, the glass, in the distance where they are, that is courage. . . . And in a difficult time like ours, when mediations are in ruins, when the tree and the stone and the fire are dangerously lacking in our life, how valuable that witness is! All Morandi's desolate discretion, closing in on the essential when the need has been measured, reveals penury. Having been warned, it is up to us to try to reinvent a hope, to begin an earth again.

Mondrian's *Red Cloud* gives to the volume its title, and *Le Nuage rouge* has in spite of its musical quality of nonreferentiality and the great harmony between its colors and refractions, a hint of divine presence and of that religious nostalgia which may linger after faith itself has been lost. The colors are those of the Virgin's blue cloak, the green of alchemy, the red of the Ideal, as Delacroix saw it, and they seem to represent our three fundamental notes. (*NR*, 117). The cloud of the color of the burning bush represents an ardor divided, accompanied by a sort of melancholy: a sign which will endure only an instant, instead of a seal which would remain placed over the work, closing it off. Less clear than most former visual epiphanies, such, for instance, as the tongues of fire pointing out the Apostles, or El Greco's sharp lightning, this cloud has interruptions of blue and white; and, unlike an iconic representation, is only the shadow of an epiphany, where a form stands out and a flame transfigures, without any reality outside or any higher code; it is at the same time as this that Mondrian paints his apple trees, those disincarnated constructions of lines and relations and number, like the music of Pythagoras, heard also by Schoenberg and Webern in Vienna. Mondrian places a horizontal and a vertical line at right angles like the symbols of the cross, the former sign of transcendence, upon his paintings, like a further proof of the attraction of the absolute, which the *Red Cloud* seemed to have gotten out of his system once and for all, and which he then censures from his canvasses. And here too another moral lesson, of a totality which may be seen to be the ultimate meaning of our own universe, revealing its light and shadow, and a glimpse of still another cloud:

We must struggle against the destruction of the lived with which all writing begins, we must then and at each instant leave the word as surely as we make it, knowing also that it is a cloud, a mass of beauties always contestable, of aspirations always to be transcended, or a vertigo, sometimes also of things torn apart, of sudden clarities. (*NR,* 122)

Mondrian's *Red Cloud* seems to show the pride of the artist's non-referential autonomy, and yet reveals also another dimension on the horizon, an "elsewhere, over there, and thus a here, in turn, that is in short, a place, which can be valid only for one life, for one duration, and forges the experience of being." Through his melancholy and his anguish, the appearance of life rejected, and of nonbelief in his writing—that *écriture* which is the very style of the canvas—Mondrian was able to keep his eyes upon the enigma. The Red Cloud, then, is the image of this enigma, and as such presides over those essays in their perception and their profundity, even in their detail.

In the chapters on poetry, commentary on language seems at first to play the predominant part: of the essay on "Words and Speech in the Song of Roland," I will have more to say in the section on "cast shadows", which treats the double structure of the medieval universe and its linguistic system, as manifested in the great epic poem. There, the realization that a living description can become a *lettre morte,* that words may seem a poor compensation for presences,

is countered by what Bonnefoy calls a "Poetry of the sentence."
Roland dies, but only from the bursting of his bronchial tubes,
"when the horn can be no more than his witness, than this object
he fills with a breath, in the universe redeemed. . . . Speech consuming itself in order to set free" (NR, 179). And such is the power
of the words that speech brings back to life that Charlemagne is
wakened by them: "And it is in this way that words are clear in
this work which its hero does not live in, but rather establishes"
(NR, 180). A return of personal poetry, even when the spiritual
instruments and symbols are lost—this kind of reality is what the
Roland essay and its companions require. All the reflections on
language hold together, against the possible hollowness of words,
in favor of their deepest function of poetry, as in love; both aim at
the cohesion and the resurrection of a universe once fragmentary
into a totality.

To take another angle on the meditations upon language, Bonnefoy's reflections on Mallarmé's poetics begin, similarly, with a
problem of presence. To speak of the "real" lake and to call it that
"pale narrow line of azure in the reeds," are these two different
things? Does it lose the density of the real object by its *excarnation*
into words? No, says Bonnefoy for Mallarmé. "Words can render
to us the earth that the earth stole from us" (NR, 186), in an
intellection and an ecstasy which are superior to any knowledge by
the concept. Poetry, again, saves experience from the common speech
in which the universe is lost, and reveals in its sacred form—for
Mallarmé, verse as the compensation for the imprecisions of speech—
a Logos, in an ambiguous *action restreinte* or limited act and action,
a serious use of and play on the reciprocal gleam words cast against
each other. In verse, as that word is taken in its most profound
sense, Idea takes form, and being is promised, in the place where
Nothingness formerly was. But chance reigns and is not abolished
by any throw of the dice, and the only being there is resides in
words. One is, then, responsible for them, and the spider of the
intellect weaves its marvelous lace, or the intricacies of thought,
within the very presence of poetry.

"Rimbaud Again," a series of answers to six questions posed by
Roger Munier, attacks those who would impose on diverse sorts of
poetry one unique model, flattening into one structure the diverse
types of possible inspiration, aspiration, forms, and substance, in
behalf of a "text." Bonnefoy speaks often on this subject and he

speaks of it convincingly as a poet and a critic: Rimbaud here opposes his posthumous refusal of such projects to the disciples of Mallarmé with their emphasis on "limited" action of the writer, in order to assert a lost dimension, that of speech taken as a presence and a summons, an *appel* in the Heideggerian sense. This, being the essential, cannot be reduced by or even touched by any model whatsoever, and goes far beyond the notion of text:

Any work which chooses itself as a text, or which one tries to interpret as a simple text, touches only the reality acquired, retains only relations between essences, registers a *state* of the relation between the consciousness and the world, and thus places itself irremediably *in the past,* even if its words contribute to the being of language. (*NR,* 215)

Rimbaud's work is, as he himself says, turned toward the future, without neglecting its origin. According to Bonnefoy, it "takes up transparency again, as the promise of a *future,* to be made by the reform of speech, and inscribes itself in history like a duty—guaranteed whatever may come by the only speech we still have, poetry" (*NR,* 216).

Rimbaud is before us and ahead of us. Bonnefoy, who in few ways resembles him, especially not his brusque rhythm or his lightning-sharp beginnings, is close to him in the silence "active in all Rimbaud said and from the beginning" (*NR,* 218). Rimbaud escapes mere "literature by his questioning and refusal, and pushes beyond mere writing, above all by asking more than he writes, by retaining his essential childishness, in which there is a lesson for all of us, for our own "illumination."

And as with the artists whom Bonnefoy sets in contrast and yet in tandem, Rimbaud has a glorious opposite whose lesson, combining with his, is still more profitable for us. Saint-John Perse, "the timeless man of the practice of things, dispossessed by the modern man given to speculation, anguish, and great industry— offers in the moment of his almost complete disappearance a poet to understand him, and to perpetuate his spirit" (*NR,* 229). He continues as a poet and a priest of nature, gathering the diverse into the law of unity: his poetry takes both science and confidence from the human gestures of work and game, and mediates the gap between nature and the destiny which is still to be built.

To the sumptuous voice of nature the arid voice of being is still opposed for us. To the happy flat country of Saint-John Perse near the sea, Rimbaud's bare place, which we can situate, never stops opposing its vertical dimension, speech like his being a summons which comes to upset our life, being also, like the initial act of the Semitic theologies, a creation *from nothing.*

And other poets who are more unlike Bonnefoy bring as much to this meditation as those who are nearer to him in feeling. One of Bonnefoy's most renowned essays concerns Pierre-Jean Jouve, a Christian writer who believes, as Bonnefoy does not, in the sullied state of the universe, and in death, not as an essential object, but as the consequence of the original fall. The tension between their attitudes, "this distance existing" between their works and experience, apparently can teach as much about being and about the function of poetry as a more visible closeness. A dualistic consciousness like that of Jouve remembers having fallen from the presence of God, but retains also a certain freedom. In a dialectical moment this lost presence is recovered as a mystery, an "astonishment painful in the ungraspable memory . . . a trace in the world of the lost presence" (*NR,* 259). In the tone of this essay, noble and anguished, one might read Bonnefoy's own criticism as poetry.

In "The Function of the Poem," which completes this section of the book, Bonnefoy reminds us that if speech is an exchange of a common consciousness, the poem simply *is* without that speaking, that common ease. It is here that he best explains what cut him off from the surrealist vision and ambition in his early twenties: surrealism put desire above reason, whereas the latter would have been necessary for any dialogue to continue, with any one or anything. His readings of Kierkegaard and Chestov in the same period taught him the importance of the relation between the self and other beings, and, implicitly and by extension, the limitations of any poetry which would turn out to be only mechanics, or have a meaning too simple. Bonnefoy's experience of poetry includes a continuity of many sudden "fractures," of opennesss, of a hold in and on the verbal substance. Any language can be put in question and can be destroyed, but can also possibly surge forth, when some stone is turned over, or some threshold is crossed. Like Parsifal, we should learn to interrogate our dreams, to show compassion and interest for and in one another, as oneiric and human keys to the poem. And cannot certain words, those whose meanings can be seen as separate from concepts, lend themselves to communion between beings, to meaning beyond a text, those words like "bread and wine," "house," "storm," and "stone"? Might this not be the kind of incarnation possible for us, in the place of the poem? "And a place will be made, of these assumptions and of these symbols which, although nothing, to be sure, in their final matter, will be our human form accomplished, and thus of unity in act and the advent of being in its absolute sense" (*NR,* 279).

In a climax to this section, Bonnefoy imagines a life spiraling deeper and deeper down, until a "new self," turned toward and present only to unity, keeping affection for objects from which words cause no separation, forming, as they do, part of the common speech. Here the union dreamed of, in the essay on Rimbaud, takes, in a further reverie, its true place as action and dream combined, existence and the body reconsidered; so the relation between self and world is reaffirmed: "Poetry does not exclude presence, it creates it, sketching out only an intelligible world and languages, and only in order to simplify them, until, on its humble bed of stars, an absolute form is born, this time one of life." Now to be sure, the hero of such a reverie does not always succeed in his aim, whether he be Parsifal or Hamlet, whether Axel or Igitur. The incarnation of an idea and the attachment to the earth and objects prevent such a perfect closure (whose shortcomings and dangers were already announced).

How can we avoid the closure of any book, its making a past of what was meant as, felt as presence? For a disaster takes place every time a writer consents to the final period. In the advent of and the sealing up of the book, under this gaze which exploits appearances, all real things situate themselves in the past, becoming finished objects. Against such a closured fate a longing for the obscure sets in, and the enigmatic is almost certain to triumph.

Yet poetry must keep the spirit of Baudelaire's "double postulation," like Flowers and Evil, the vertical and the horizontal, angel and devil: leaning at once toward Mallarmé's "limited action," coordinating and cohering, and toward the disquieting voices of the dream, holding those contradictory attitudes: "the function of the poem will have been to be divided from itself, to feel the uselessness of even its formal being. And this already, at the heart of a finitude not chosen but suffered, filtering from everywhere through the half-closed door, assures some presence to the voice maintaining itself in a book" (*NR,* 283).

The final section of the book contains essays on unity, even in the beginning sentence of the essay of Paul Celan and his life. Perhaps Celan took his life as he did so that "for once words would coincide with what is." Celan, always an outsider by his Jewish heritage, a German-speaking poet in Paris, bears a memorable witness to the fallacious facility of culture: "Our words are often simply a cloud [again the *nuée* and the *nuage* as image], cast as a structure over what we call the universe." And the doubt of our century, the poverty of feeling and the shallowness apparent in all that is around us, are faced straight on by the painters and writers dear to Bonnefoy. Each gesture matters: the light or the dark or the back-lighting of some canvas, hope or despair, coherence or disarray.

"Nothing but black against white on the page, and already all the decisions of the ethical resound, and all the foliage of words." (*NR*, 322). A canvas can, for instance, invite us to some table laden with fruits, where our disquiet will be calmed. It is a matter of the simplest things; details which might have seemed trivial now take upon them and within them a remarkable fullness.

Oh, it is not so little! And the world could perfectly well finish, absurdly, by not understanding the value, for the only real search, of the smell of damp grass nearby, of an ant scurrying across the page, of an owl's cry at the door suddenly lighting up a sign still sealed. (*NR*, 326)

In conclusion, there is a hope: that the earth once taken from us may begin its second existence. In the essay "Second Earth," in the place where we have learned to work together in and over this land of poetry, there shines a cloud, as universal as in Buddhist thought, as meaningful as Mondrian's red one, as enigmatic as a cloud of writing. Bonnefoy's image leads the reader back to the problem of the sign formerly touched upon: "How can we interpret, in the failure of so many signs? The traveler has entered a labyrinth. The desert is a threshold to him, exalting, and which he has never ceased to traverse" (*NR*, 329).

And yet, Bashô's path, that of the Buddhist faith, narrow and winding, seems to lead to everything, everywhere. But between Mallarmé and Bashô, shall we have to choose as between "speech desiring and unable to establish, and this language offering itself?" (*NR*, 334). Could we not refuse the generalities we as Westerners are used to—relying as we usually do on concepts—and cling instead to the transcendence of the subject we are, and our specificity, keeping clear in us this "shining cloud?" Could we not adapt the attitude that words are not made "to reach the *in-itself* of things, but to deepen the relationship between a presence and a place?" (*NR,* 339).

We might have then the emptiness Bashô perceives, not that distance of some of the languages and conceptual systems of our day, but a feeling for the earth, kept and intensified. We could ask of each word its use; what it nourishes. Then, unlike Parsifal, we might learn to ask the saving question, and in time. This essay on "La Nuée" or the cloud, ends—and it is an appropriate ending for this present section—with a summons made to our mind and judgment, with a desire that they be endowed with calm lucidity and penetrated by hope: "to weigh, in words, colors, and sounds, what is bread and wine—what is cloud—and to separate it from what is ashes" (*NR,* 345).

Reading The Cast Shadows: A Reflection

> To care for the cast shadows,
> surely, and to care for nothing
> else. . . .
> "L'Humour, les ombres portées" [*URM,* 37]

Shadow Against Light. For Mallarmé, Bonnefoy reminds us, the noblest function is that ascribed to the sense of sight: the following comments are meant merely as a sighting taken on Bonnefoy's own vision, a more-than-modest homage to his illumination and the necessary shadows which clarify it, however paradoxically. In a general lighting, the shadows cast by specific objects in their opaque resistance are irrevocably associated with a present and with a presence: "What the cast shadow profoundly designates . . . is *a certain place at a certain moment . . .*" (*URM,* 36). The reality of encounter, lit as it is and shadowed, entails an ontological imperfection, for nothing we know is fully lit. Insofar as the shadows retain the trace of even the most tenuous aspects of being—the odd profile of a top hat or an ox's horn as it prolongs the shadow of an angel's guitar, for example, in a Piero della Francesca—they represent the opposite pole to the orangerie, that perfect place of light and form, unlivable but all the more present to the thought.

Such shadows are linked both to presence and to anguish, that of the essential cleavage in the object and in the instant, of the eternal absence of a key to understanding, especially in that country beyond, that *Arrière-Pays* just on the other side of our sight. Here the poet is moved to a dark vision, and, as elsewhere, the sun appears black from it, and the land, suddenly bare: "if real life is over there, in that elsewhere with no place to it, that is enough for the land here to take on the aspect of a desert" (*AP,* 21). Nerval's blackest sun casts its own shadows here, in a terrible prolongation, and Hölderlin's *Hyperion* too, while, closer to us, de Chirico's hyperlengthened forms take a terrible and specific hold on our consciousness, attached as they are to "a glove, a mannequin, or a piece of fruit, elementary objects in which the reflection of an arcade's columns is effaced forever" (*SS,* 37).

To this fullness, lost suddenly, the poetic spirit reacts violently. For the reader in turn, the importance of a dark spot seen on the sun cannot be overestimated: to this reader, the poet has communicated his greatest gift, his own "ardent melancholy," and the richness is incalculable. It is not always by a good light that one can best read, but sometimes by a shadow, providing that shadow is clearly seen, significantly placed, and essential to the understanding.

The reader on whose experience these shadows are cast may well give another sense to the expression "ombres portées," these cast shadows being cast or "portées" in all their terrible dark glory before the attentive vision. Not as some casual interruption of the whiteness of a Mallarméan page to be contrasted with the print marking it, but rather as a sign, irreversibly natural and specifically sensible to mind and eye. (If the qualification "sensible" appears with frequency in Bonnefoy's essays, holding in itself both the attributes of the tangible and the sensed, it is the indication of an intelligence sharply conscious of the intensity of the real there before us.) This consciousness finds itself visually intensified by these shadows of the specific object, fixed and yet assuming different stages in their overwhelming presence. "Our painting is the place of shadows" (*NR,* 52), says Bonnefoy in an essay on Balthus, and this statement must be read against its basic mental backdrop, an evident luminous faith in shadow's opposite: "I believe, for example, in light" (*AP,* 23).

Thus the fascination of the baroque which marks Bonnefoy's own vision, sometimes strongly. The art of the baroque tends often toward a most serious play of light and dark, and such a chiaroscuro rendering casts its own shadow and its own illumination into the reading of painting and text. The hope of the present reading is that some of that complexity and depth can be rendered with shadow as the starting point.

Ripeness and Ruin. Bonnefoy's recent essay on Shakespeare's *Lear* and *Hamlet,* an extraordinary play upon two words in the two plays, uses just such contrast for its tones, both visual and sounded, whose depth and interrelations are mutually enhanced by the correspondence. So *Lear* is read against and with *Hamlet* as bright zones correspond to the dark which they complement, or positive to negative images in photography. To Hamlet's "something is rotten" there responds a mysterious prideful sickness of the soul, in a state not exterior, but interior; Hamlet's "readiness is all," in its acceptance of chance in a world destructive and stripped of sense, is still present for the audience hearing or seeing Edgar's "ripeness is all," that act of faith made directly in the face of Hamlet's despairing doubt. "We learn," says Shakespeare's best and most poetic translator, "that the structures of meaning are only a bridge of thread cast over the horrendous abyss, but that its strands are of steel" (*H,* 22). As "ripeness," a sign of unity and of a full response to a full meaning, replaces Hamlet's call to a simple "readiness," empty of sense in a senseless world, so light takes its source from a preceding shadow, and the grass grows once more among the ruins (*H,* 27).

As an example of what a cast shadow of a past text might represent in an individual reading, I hear in this image of grass and of its regrowth among the ruins a line coming to the traveler who is the poet, falling upon the stones at Arezzo in *L'Arrière-Pays,* surely the most impassioned land of poetry: "But the grass is always the same" (*AP,* 82). And then the traveler, refreshed and reilluminated, starts his travels once more. This luminous moment, epiphanic and echoing, whose new forms are identical in essence and yet reborn, serves as a telescoping of the two texts, as a shadow for the journey between specific stone and stone as ornament or then idea; such a shadow mediates between stone and ruin, between individual leaf and general nature: it connects and joins, echoes, prolongs, and renders real at last. Finally, each reader's presence, silent and only supposed,

casts its interpretive shadow subsequently through the work, haunting and transmissible in its dark tones, infinitely sensitive.

Place of Reflection. I maintain that the shadow is not only
exterior, is not cast merely as a horizontal darkness, but more gravely,
as the deeply sensed anguish of finitude, rending the heart and
separating the partial being from its full potentiality: "Something
touches me so that being is cloven apart, with its light, and I am
in exile" (*AP*, 24). At the sensed summit of vision, shadow does
not cover all the space of earth; rather, it renders present the conscious poetic journey and its real dimension of effort, giving its true
worth to "the real place." Not the one *lieu* in the Greek formula of
true place, where each object was given in its right and proper
situation, but the notion as Bonnefoy conceives it, made of exile
and of night, based on darkness, accepting the imperfection of its
own undoing by time: the cast shadow holds its metaphysical place
as its right and due: "Happy, those men of the rising sun if they
can, like Piero della Francesca, find their footing in a wisdom, but
far truer, those men of shadow" (*SS*, 39).

The baroque movement, upon which Bonnefoy often comments,
reaffirms the object, sensible and specific, and fated, within its
absolute and undying form, reaffirms, against the Greek daylight,
another reign. It is illuminated this time in a temporal and only
partially tragic perspective: "The baroque loves and transsubstan-
tiates what is limited and passes by . . ." (*AP*, 150). Baudelaire's
sonnet "À une passante" resounds again in the mind, with its figure
of the unknown passerby all the more desirable for her elusiveness:
"You whom I would have loved. . . ." So Bonnefoy's *Arrière-Pays*,
that country beyond but also here, responds with its mystery intact;
and for all its vivid imperfection, it alone reveals the setting in
which we might live. The nearby place of existence assumed, which
is the place of shadow and of earth, is also and forever the place of
reflection, and thus also the place of the reader, created by his own
perception: "But if our readings were to dream us?" (*AP*, 127).

Reading in the Dusk. In a castle, one empty music room
where nothing is any longer heard except in the memory, is now a
place of mingled peace and pain, "the altar in its afternoon of shadow
gathering all the remaining hope of meaning, all thought of *place,*
the only value prevailing against the drift of *signs*" (*RT*, 51). This
dark afternoon glimpsed in *Rue traversière* returns the reader to the
few lines from *Rome 1630,* in which Bonnefoy defines the baroque

gesture and its importance for our understanding: here the dusk of a chapel provides a dim light proper to an inner perception:

the baroque is not a visual deception, but rather an experience of being through illusion . . . so we see that what the baroque suggests is not of the nature of the senses, because it concerns our relation with being, our adherence to fate: and from that it follows that its most intense moments may be, in the dusk of a chapel, some painted plaster figurine, some Neapolitan saint totally unknown, but bearing on her forehead a crown of roses or paper, or a tiny light. (*R,* 39–40)

The exterior sign, often trivial, may nevertheless mediate between us and the essential, entirely and efficaciously; but the dream of poets goes beyond mere surface and sensation to a possible convergence some day of absence and presence, to the hope of a true place where shadow will be implicated forever in light.

In his reflections on literature, this hope motivates a series of subtle readings of myth and of text. So, for instance, the contrary forces in the *Song of Roland* are seen to vivify one another: the Saracens are pitted against the French, Roland against Oliver, to be sure, but also French against French, Roland against Roland: "Against whom do we ever struggle if not our double? Against this *other* in us which would convince us that the world has no meaning, which would have us, wounded and deprived of hope, turn toward the stream where the blood of the ending day drains away, from the lost battle?" Of all things, the most terrible is not just meaninglessness (for it at least has color, "as with the red of a victory or a loss") but rather "the indifference of everything that is, its resonance like an empty jar."

In the war on indifference, the landscape is sensed in its contrary possibilities: here transparency and clarity are played against their opposite: "From the trees to the emperor, from abundance to duty, through great transparent words arches God's presence. And nothing unexplored, nothing future. Except those 'high dark mountains' over there, on the southern border. . . ." Of this landscape Bonnefoy says that it is space itself, and depth and luminous hierarchy, but within that limpid world he has us glimpse a fierce unease. "I look gladly at these trees of the first day, these 'shining stars,' this 'clear' night—everything is at peace, it seems, in the depth of nature, but why this troubled voice, which speaks to us of an evil always begun anew?"

The question itself as it is posed forms the shadow for the splendid structure like an army in its moral call to war, the enemy is able to transfer the sign from one side to the other. Were he to win, would the sun and trees not alter, from horror rather than from hatred? Would they not from then on be absurd forms and a "black sun?" The landscape shifts, then, with the drama it contains, even if finally that drama is enacted by two opposing sides within the self.

But as for the enemy, hidden in ourselves, he is further proof of an architecture of the same, not of same and other. Beyond the political and personal and psychological structure, we find the mirror imagery of one side set over against the other even within the same element. The dark echoes once more against the light, shadow against certainty. The question persists, with is implied positive answer: "What then is the evil that menaces this harmony? And from what exterior space might it come? There is no exterior to a form which appropriates the real, no *other* conceivable in the architecture of the *same*. Then why this moral rearming in the song against an "Infidel"? And if evil has its own structure, is it not hidden, in one way or another, already within the fair dwelling in which we live?"

Risk. Evil, like shadow, puts the object in question, challenging its obvious evidence: this is the passing shadow or the moment of greatest risk: "A terrible moment: this must be emphasized. For without anything having changed, everything may lose its value. . . . What can one construct, on what can one base one's action . . . if even the orchard can signify the desert?" And then, too, significance is nothing without substance. Words are insufficient and we need the presences of which they are only traces, which they cannot bring back to life; and for life, intelligibility cannot substitute: "A 'world' is nothing in itself. The same key for the same door, the same labors as yesterday going on around one . . . above all and everywhere the same galaxy of values, of tastes, of connivences or conflicts with the distant and the near, and all of that in the rustling of familiar presences—all that can change suddenly, without changing its form, all life vanish when just one link gives out, which supported all the others. . . ."

Absence is just on the other side of the mental landscape: "And how to find again what will have disappeared?" The waste land is perhaps the most basic metaphor of all the song and legend accompanying the noble scene, as a shadow deepens a sight: the latter is my concern here. There is joined to it, moreover, the knowledge that the French landscape of the *Song of Roland,* for example, is pervaded not just by the dark of a Saracen night, but by an inner betrayal, undoing the French tongue: "Guenes i vint, ki la traisun fist. / Des or (e) commencet le cunseill que mal prist" ("Ganelon then came, who did the treason. / Then began the counsel which went wrong"). This is the division from within, inescapable.

But Roland dies and thereby reinvents sacrifice; he destroys the boundary of those "high dark mountains." The landscape takes on the poetry of fate, as heroic possibility joins with the certainty of death:

While Roland fights, we become aware that things are transformed—a change of horizon, a slippage of these real mountains, of these armies, into the space of a consciousness, a transmutation of the event into symbol, of the memory into a poem. In this theater of Roncevaux, which will become eternal thereby—a "spiritual battle" as Rimbaud will say—everything is from now on interior, as in the creation (or the contemplation) of an icon.

Roland is always conscious not only of honor, but of death. (In a recent French film of the *Chanson de Roland,* the fourteenth-century pilgrims shown wandering and celebrating nightly the song itself are nevertheless dubious as to the role of Roland itself. Klaus Kinsky, the actor playing the pilgrim who plays Roland also inveighs against the role, calling it a Song of Death.) And speaking of Roland, Bonnefoy speaks of salvation and shadow: "he knows full well that what saves from death is the acceptance of death. . . . By virtue of Roland, the dark is only virtual in the work. . . . The waters of presence take form again."

Finally, in the rereading of the shadow, a passage from *Dans le leurre du seuil* (In the lure of the threshold) reveals luminous doubt and dark certainty, just as does the song Roland sings. Here the obscurity of a wandering and of grief together confront the lucid resolution to understand; here, as on the high pass of some mountain, the moment of convergence is only suggested by the poem itself, like a song of defeat and triumph heard or sung on some threshold between day and death:

Et tant vaut la journée qui va finir,
Si précieuse la qualité de cette lumière,
Si simple le cristal un peu jauni
De ces arbres, de ces chemins parmi des sources,
Et si satisfaisantes l'une pour l'autre
Nos voix, qui eurent soif de se trouver
Et ont erré, côte à côte, longtemps
Interrompues, obscures. (*P*, 290–91)

(And so fine the day about to end,
So precious the quality of this light,
So simple the slightly yellowed crystal
Of these trees, of these paths among the springs,
And how our voices satisfy
After thirsting each for the other
And have long wandered side by side
Interrupted and obscure.)

Lack and Limit.   To accept the art of shadow entails, first, the acknowledgment of incompleteness, of a piece with the imperfection Bonnefoy cherishes: "I remember the first page was missing" (*AP*, 85). So the beginning is missing, and with it, the reader and writer's natural hope for a text entire—for a Book, Mallarmé's *Livre*—in its impossible and absolute completion. The true place is elsewhere, and more open: "It is in my becoming, which I can keep open, and not in the closed text. . . . It must be the crucible where, once dissipated, the country beyond takes new form. And where a few words, finally, will shine perhaps, simple and transparent like the nothing of language, still everything and real" (*AP*, 149). And these few words, radiant as they are real, take the place of the former absolutes, now in fullness and knowledge. Simple and sufficient, sure as the shadows of some larger hope, they link as with threads or lines of steel the two shores of the abyss Shakespeare sensed. Here, as in the Renaissance paintings in whose counter light Bonnefoy's essays can be seen sometimes to stand, time joins with the timeless, perspective with fate.

Specific present is joined by language to specific past. As the words of Mallarmé form the cross-reflections of his "feux-croisés," glancing off each other in their multiple facets, so these shadows too reflect upon and measure each other, as they reflect and measure the objects casting them originally in their roles, never without some measureless mystery. Against a profile closed in its sharp definition, shadow might well signify this unknowing, the paradoxical sureness of uncertainty, and the quivering openness of what might be. Against certainty and closure, we would choose the passing poetry whose intensity dapples bright with black, sun with shade.

Cloud, Leaf, and Sign. As into negative theologies light is cast from beneath and above ("lumière d'en-dessous, d'au-dessus" [*NR,* 73]), so now the shadows are cast vertically as the necessary precedent for and companion of the crimson sun. From Bonnefoy's thoughts on Mondrian to his essays gathered under the sign of a red cloud, *Nuage rouge,* that single image holds in and balances the art of shadow by its own triumphant color, as in the art of the baroque, black and red are balanced against each other.

As for the threshold—that threshold stressing the idea of boundary for some country beyond, separating here from there and yet joining them—it begins as if by an answer to an unspoken question. What of the shadow of time falling now across the poet's path and setting its limit, and ours, and our measure: is it too to be accepted, unprotestingly? "Yes," the threshold poem begins, and it is one of the great long poems of our century, to be placed alongside the "Waste Land" of Eliot, and Stevens' "Rock" and Tzara's "Approximate Man," these markers of our epoch. But to return to our own question, what of the shadow cast across the threshold, what of the lack, what of the sign fallen silent?

The monumental essay "Baudelaire against Rubens" bears the answer, again prefaced by the positive "Yes," a yea-saying devoid of sentimentality, and perhaps a partial clue to the crimson cloud, a positive and prolonged response: "Redness, yes, of the God of yesteryear, that lack, that writing consequently a death—but in the dark fire a transparency, the God to be born who is no one and will be nothing, shining nevertheless on the farm roof over there transfigured, shining here in several words redeemed" (*NR,* 73). And in those words redeemed we hear others, heard also in the *Arrière-Pays,* the simple and transparent words "which will be, however, everything" and "real." There too, the triumphant assurance of the "nevertheless" rules, resurrecting and restoring faith. The radiance of the redemption is further illuminated by the modesty of the tone and the qualifications sensed in the vocabulary and the vision, those limits the shadows, explicit or implicit, forever mark.

Last, in a most humble object already seen to be more real and closer in its imperfection still than any yet seen, in that one torn and dirtied leaf of ivy, we find a truer representation of the human consciousness than any unwithered brilliance could offer; there the wounded presence of poetry finds its real place, full of shadow and darkened by passing time:

I shall say, allegorically, it is this fragment of the somber tree, this broken leaf of ivy. The entire leaf, building its immutable essence from all its veinings, would already be the concept. But this broken leaf, green and black, dirtied, this leaf revealing in its wound all the depth of what is, this infinite leaf is pure presence and consequently my salvation. Who could take from me its having been mine, and in a contact beyond destinies and sites, within the absolute? Who could destroy it, already destroyed? (*I*, 28–29)

And the shadow cast bears the same witness to a wounded presence as the torn leaf, being the same indication of human vision and of human art, in its multiplicity of ambivalent signs and of contradictory signals. What reader of contemporary poetry—what dweller in contemporary time—could not say, with Bonnefoy: "It is clear that we have long wandered, and doubted, among the signs" (*NR*, 353)? The going has never been less easy, less certain, less absolute, for the wanderers along poetic ways.

Words need, says Bonnefoy, a grid through which to be seen, and it is "our chance, our own place, our existence . . ." (*URM*, 23). Our chance might well be this quite simple one, made of light, but just as surely, of shadow, made of the far and the near. "What shall we use as a grid for seeing? The representation of earth and sky because the country beyond is first of all a gaze upon the place nearby?" Our outward vision might well merge with the deepest and most private of insights, the nearest place, not the least tragic, but the most radiant, that poetry alone provides.

To grasp in full consciousness the paradox—that is, dark as the measure of clarity, and imperfection as the measure of presence—is perhaps to bring, as Bonnefoy says of the *Chanson de Roland,* a language back to life. After so much textual science, the word as shadow might now be revalued, in quiet and searchingly. For it is in the depth of these silent inner shadows that we must at present and at last reread the work of Bonnefoy, in reflection, and in their light.

Art has taken place, and we are saved. (*RT,* 35).

Chapter Four

Crossroads and the Country Beyond

Bonnefoy's understated autobiography *L'Arrière-Pays* (The country beyond, 1972), is a moving meditation on the landscape of art, memory, and the imagination. His own life and the life of the mind merge in the country always behind the one in which we live and read and see now, at once implicated in what is here, and yet always recessed in its memory, with its past folded into the present, and the presence deeper for its haunting.

"No one would walk there as though he were in a foreign land" (*AP,*7). This sentence, which Bonnefoy quotes from Plotinus about the One, defines the dream of "the country beyond." The crossroads of two paths seems best to reveal that land, always behind or beyond, of which Robert Frost would have said, "The road not taken." Such meditation provides less matter for regret than for curiosity about that other land and that other way—curiosity not because the climate or the landscape would be remarkable, but because, quite simply, it is not and cannot be *here,* and that realization may take away some savor from the present land.

Now dissatisfaction does not imply not loving the earth, or not finding it sufficient. But just at the moment when this earth is apparently enough—"Here, in the promise, is the place"—the idea of the Other Country takes hold. A key to some mystery seems to be lacking in the present, which we know we cannot dominate or overlook. Looking at or imagining the other place, we suspect it of somehow containing the answer to the riddle—or to the apparent meaninglessness—of this place, if we were only to see it. It is *there* we would walk un-strangely, whereas here we shall, perhaps, always be in exile, with no reason as to why, and even no definition for the here, except as not-the-other. This volume is nevertheless meant to be the reconciliation of the here as the *true place* and the here as the *not-there.* Such a tension gives a peculiar and lyric fascination to this work, which of all Bonnefoy's essays seems to us the strongest and the most coherent. The question posed in it, and the anguish visible, seem to touch the heart of the matter, in the text as in the life it absorbs and which, finally, absorbs it:

Yes, it is true, our country is lovely, I cannot imagine anything else, I am at peace with this language, my distant god has only withdrawn a few steps, the epiphany is simple: still if true life is over there, in that elsewhere which cannot be situated, that alone suffices for the here to take on the aspect of a desert. . . . Here there is only a lack, whose grandeur is a desire, whose frequentation is an exile. . . . Truly, something has only to touch me—and that can be the most humble thing . . . for being to cleave apart, in its light, and for me to be in exile. (24)

It is again a question of the crucial importance of understanding and of the words attached to it in Bonnefoy's work, where it serves as a key to his own writing and thinking; the curiosity about the other land and about comprehending it applies also to this one. Vigilance is aroused, and the mind is always on watch. A light has only to be seen from some train at evening, and the questions surge forth: "What is the name of those villages over there? why the gleam on the terrace: who among us is being signaled, who is being summoned?" (15). Of course, were one to arrive, the curiosity would be extinguished, and thus the country over there would become the country here, having no longer its enchantment. The loss, then, is double; we lose this land and also that one, once we have arrived there, forsaking the here. The deception with the here—and, as we have seen, eventually with the over-there, once awareness has taken root—is deep, convincing, and moving. It touches all that man finds to value: speech as well as matter, sign as well as substance: "There is a discourse among men, a ceaseless speaking, but is it not just as vain and repetitive as the sea foam, the sand or all those vacant stars? How pitiful is the sign!" (24).

But we must also bear in mind that our "side of the mountain" is not just, or not simply "disposessed," in behalf of the other side: "What leaves in spirit remains in body. . . . nothingness as insistent as it is paradoxical" (29). This world returns, and is given a new structure and a new meaning by the unknown, a *second presence,* participating in a more interior relation with the self.

Since the obsession with that other land is sensed only at certain moments, at the metaphorical crossroads of life, and not in our daily occupations, it is no threat to the latter, but rather an enlargement of our horizon. We are set in a "double postulation" between there and here: that expression reminds us that Baudelaire's own double postulation was toward heaven and hell, saint and devil, hope and despair, whereas the two tendencies of Bonnefoy, opposed in a different way, will find their reconciliation, unlike the contraries of Baudelaire. Bonnefoy here recounts the moments, in childhood and after, when and where the *Arrière-Pays* seemed nearest and most troubling, in the stories and paintings illustrating the volume, all of which seem endowed with a sense of miracle.

Words as well as landscapes, stories told as well as places and monuments seen, may serve as doors to the "other side." A story familiar from childhood is recounted, and in sympathy with its hero, but in contrast with him the narrator of this autobiography finds self-definition through the other. The details of the particular story matter less than the psychological discovery to which it leads:

> For I know perfectly well what makes me different from that man who sought and found. He desired his true place so as to consume there a life which he knew to be, even there, an entrapment for the earth. He meant only to take up there, once again, the interrupted quest for total deliverance. And I, caring about transcendence but also about a place where it would have its roots, it is on this latter, a "vain matter," that I conferred the quality of the absolute. (45)

Pride should not lead us to situate the country here at hand as the center of things; but the obsessive quest for another place than this should not exile us from this one, into an absolute departure which would lose the present and what is close-at-hand. In the privileged moments where the possible crossroads is found, its description takes on a completely different tone, nearer to that of the poems: "A place and the visible evidence have been identified, here and elsewhere are no longer opposed . . . presence, the very fact of the earth in its roundness produces a place. . . . Existence rose direct like a smoke which no wind could divert. I am convinced . . . " (53). For whatever reason we might think of, or need, an elsewhere, however we might feel ourselves unfulfilled, an alliance can be, must be, made with the "ici périssable," the here which will perish: the roads of departure and of return must be left open.

In an extraordinary fashion, the illustrations—art works and figures, landscapes of mountains and plains—heighten the tone. The poet examines this art and this countryside now brought near to hand with an eye and a spirit for the elsewhere, comparing the artists open to the thought of the latter with those opposed to it. Uccello, for instance, seems to render all things exterior and to place all events and colors at a distance, to present all forms as fantastic, so that he lacks simple beauty, whereas, at least before the author's revelatory visit to Italy, de Chirico seemed to refer to an elsewhere only in an unreality which appeared to deny ordinary temporality, even his shadows being too long for the objects associated with them: "I was dreaming, as I said, of another world. But I wanted it to be of flesh and time, like ours, and such that one could live there, change one's age there, and die there" (62).

Yet the splendor of Italian painting is that this other world, and the interiority of the object, as well as the unity of the real and of the sacred, are indeed found in the early painters: Giotto, Piero della Francesca, Masaccio, who define a place of rebirth. There Bonnefoy's prolonged and determined battle against the exile from the flesh or *excarnation* is renewed. Troubling questions arise on his visit to Italy: does the affirmation of these painters remain merely intellectual? Does "some excess of appearance" in them not stress the same unrest that we feel in de Chirico, at the expense of presence which is founded principally upon the invisible?

For some time this doubt is felt to haunt the book, which takes part of its appeal from its very windings and questioning, from assurances challenged once more. Bonnefoy's reexaminations of this subject cannot be resumed, but only pointed to as exemplary of a deeply subtle and poetic thought expressed in prose. He finds that our knowing is founded not on the reproduction of appearances, but on the struggle between the strongly felt immediate nd the yearned after transcendent, just as his own struggle between the here and the elsewhere produces the very work being read: "Nothing is really immediate, nothing even exists, everything is earned during the course of a life, and first of all, the beauty of the place which it assumes" (79).

The voyage to be made in writing is no other than the one made in painting, and can profit from the observation of the latter: in a ruined painting or fresco, the stripping of the exterior by time and finitude reveals the interior form whose traces the painter may have lost in the color and the outer contours. It is as if a voice were to say: "I efface what I write, you see, because you have to read" (84).

In some sense, the *Arrière-Pays* is the story of a traveler who has destroyed the story of a traveler, as Bonnefoy did. This remarkable book tells and exorcises that other story, making of it an interior voyage by the destruction of the tale of an exterior one. "I ripped up *The Traveler* because I no longer wanted an imaginative writing, sealed off from reality, but an analysis fully aware, the condition necessary for moral experience" (100). At this point the confrontation in Bonnefoy's childhood of two regions of France—represented by Tours where he spent his winters, and Toirac where he spent his summers and where his family had its origins—lend their mythical and nostalgic dimensions to the interior struggle: the plenitude and openness of summer, the closed shutters and desolation of winter, after the war, and then, the effort at transcendence of this earthly space. In the fullness of the summer dwelling and the fruits of the golden days, there were small signs like signals of the other and darker side of things: an iron bridge under the poplars, a pool of oil, images found again in his poems. One tree with its isolated profile, seemingly deprived of meaning, is associated with the fact of loneliness, for it enters his consciousness first at the death of his grandparents: this is the first marker between the visible and the infinite. Traces of this experience remain scattered throughout his other work: in this present volume are to be found the keys for much of Bonnefoy's own "elsewhere."

Between whatever center one chooses—Rome, for instance, toward which Bonnefoy's early study of Latin led, and the country beyond it, or Apecchio, the place one passes by—there are multiple realizations in the concrete world of the ambiguity sketched here. Is there a special kind of truth found here, and would it be his own kind of truth? Might one prefer the beauty of a work of art—and this is the question to be finally answered—to that of experience lived? This is a grave question, for "I saw correctly that such a choice, giving words over to themselves, making from them a language, created a universe which would assure to the poet *everything:* except that in separating himself from the openness of days, misunderstanding time and other people, he was really leaning toward nothing but solitude" (120–21). The last part of the book considers this problem and this final warning of the poet to himself.

A return to Italy rounds off the quest and the finding, and not without ambiguity, as indeed one would have expected. As the arrival before in Italy had been signaled by the arcades of de Chirico, the return is marked by a Sphinx at Delphi; "What, after all, does it see? Stable forms or infinite metamorphosis? Or rather, does it not mingle them in a new vision, in an absolute gaze?" (130). Or again, does it not represent an equation? For Bonnefoy was trained as a mathematician and his early mathematical meditations included the borderlines between finite and infinite; these images remain, with their associations of the known and the unknown. He considers, for instance, that "the Sphinx was the equation where there figured a definite relation of spatial knowledge to wisdom, of intelligible beauty to another. Or then, the image of the infinite sea set against the finite contour of Venice. . . . Furthermore, along these lines, when the poet is tempted to write another story about the unknown, as a double to *Le Voyageur,* entitled 'un sentiment inconnu,' it will not be written down. For to write it would be to betray the very indications given or granted. 'The earth *is,* the word *presence* has a meaning. And the dream is too . . . ' " (149). A dream, however, must not be written but lived. For then, "knowing itself the dream, it becomes simplified, and the earth comes about, little by little."

This is the lesson, finally, that Poussin teaches us at the conclusion of *L'Arrière-Pays:* for he tried to combine numbers and the real, the infinite and the finite, however vain any such attempt must be. And yet, finally, he picks up one clot of earth "and says it is Rome," thus making of his great canvasses, such as *Moses Saved,* what Bonnefoy makes of his own words: the salvation of the here and the now, imbued with the unsatisfied longing for an elsewhere. Both of these, the near and the far understood, make the work and save the real, transfigured, as is language, by this understanding.

It is in my becoming, which I can keep open, and not in the closed text, that this vision, this nearby thought, must be inscribed and flourish, and come to fruit, if it has, as I believe it to, meaning for me. It will be the crucible where the country beyond, having been dissipated, will be re-formed, where the vacant *here* will be crystallized. And where perhaps a few words, finally, will become radiant, although simple and transparent like the nothingness of language, so that nevertheless they will be everything, and real. (89)

Chapter Five
Conclusion: Poetry as Sojourn

> evil will not have existed,
> or not for long . . .
> (*Entretiens sur la Poésie* [1981])

For this "constructor of countries beyond, ceaselessly begun afresh," rebeginning is always possible, despair always limited by hope. Bonnefoy's great essay entitled "The Act and the Place of Poetry" is dedicated to the optimistic desire of "reuniting poetry and hope . . . ": not the oblivion to death which would be only a refusal to see its necessary coming, not the compensatory divine which might be posited to make up for our certain failure of possession; not even a central impulse toward knowledge or gnosis, a temptation strongly sensed in his work—but a hope based on words and the word, on the giving of what they alone can give, and a desire centered in poetry as that giving: "I have no doubt that modern poetry—poetry without gods—should know what it desires so as to judge, in full knowledge, the power of words. . . . "

This form of desire necessarily remains desire; this form of possession by the act of poetry remains, no less so, tinged by dispossession. The essay ends with the great ambivalence which we recognize in Bonnefoy's most haunting works of poetry and prose: "I am thinking of the poet of the most vivid hope and the most vital sadness," he concludes, calling the poet's most valuable gift that of an ardent melancholy, communicated in a generosity which is a true richness amid the apparent poverty in which he lives. The tone of Bonnefoy's most deeply poetic essays conveys just that richness, exemplified in the concluding image of this one which celebrates sight and concomitant emotion, understating the whole for an interrogative statement all the more moving: should not the light of the sun setting, reflected in the window of some hut on the side of some mountain suffice?

Suffice for what? This question never arises, and that in itself is significant. The presence felt, of the world and the light in it that we love, by the viewer who needs its signs and its sights, is enough to guarantee a sojourn here and now. In this indwelling imagination, the most modest mountain hut and the most formal orangerie somehow find their poetic junction. The solitude or "esseulement" of the poet guarantees, with the sense of another presence still now to come, an interiority as rich as the gift of sharing.

Guarantees, also, a faith, not in the religions which have left us, but in faith itself, always indefinable as it is always future and yet present right here, right now: "Life structures what it finds outside of itself, and the world enlarges and deepens, from age to age, this inscription and form: we might call it the earth . . . " (*E,* 152).

It is this, finally, beyond the limits of the image or even the symbol, that forms the forward and wide-ranging impulse which Bonnefoy gives us, from his own attitude as it is turned toward the "authentic terrestrial sojourn." The poem, reflecting us, is never perfection but the road of an effort, quiet despite the clamor outside it, useless in a world made pragmatic by long tradition, and therefore free to show a certain modesty of means and of goal: Bonnefoy's poetry will not be seen as having aimed for the epic, although it often attains it; it should be seen rather as the constantly unified parts of a long and continuous sense of personal place and of care beyond the personal.

Poetry was always to have been, in fact and in large part, a great caring for a place and a tongue which would speak of the community of readers as of the self. The smallest gestures indicate the deepest thoughts, bringing them among us:

Bringing in the wash, chopping the wood, sweeping up at midnight the hearth's ashes, each act, in this mental space . . . is like cleaning the windows of a perfect house of light wood and glass, or placing in the middle of it a few flowers and resuming it all: after which you can rise from the long care of a place which is the word to take it all in with one look. . . . (*H,* x)

Poetry is finally the most essential one of those places mentioned in his essay on "Haiku," which seem "made to retain the absolute in our presence as a fire is preserved between the stones of some hearth." This retention of one aspect of things or of the overall

reality inserted between lesser elements, to be guarded and to be
perceived, is paralleled, I think, by the voice of the other, the
other's consciousness as Bonnefoy keeps it within the poetry of the
self. What is essential may be called the presence of the self to
the other and of the other to the self: as he puts it in "Baudelaire
Conversing with Mallarmé," one of his *Entretiens sur la poésie,* "the
other needed in his profound difference, his freedom, so that our
form can have access to his meaning. The consciousness of the other
is the way of incarnation, the deciphering of the real" (*E,* 91).

Language, he says in another interview, is not be be limited to
description, but rather is to be extended toward the other, in order
to found together a place, and to "decide its meaning" (*E,* 21).
Beyond and between the symbols of poetry—those dense moments
containing the synthesis of all feeling and meaning—and the mar-
gins left about them, is the real truth of poetry, sensed only at the
crossroads of the two beings, myself writing and the other reading—
or, as we might say in our present optic—between myself reading
and the other writing, whatever the name with which the text is
signed. "To write poetically is, it seems to me, to speak, no matter
how poorly, the language of the other" (*E,* 36). This is the partial
answer to the requirements of self and poetry and world and relation,
the reason for returning to writing, always, after unwriting. For
returning toward a speech that will be the extension of the self to
the other, and then to a crossroads where still more is joined, in
this universe built by and for the poetic word:

Saying "I" should no longer betray the arrogance of the "self," but quite
simply the act of knowledge found in its most natural place, the source
of both illusion and lucidity. May it grope finally toward the reality of
an "us," under the stars, even if the path which is bound to lead us far
on . . . should be ceaselessly obstructed by avalanches, by our own shortcomings, and by the various forms of noise that poetry cannot master.
(*NR,* 76)

The note is modest, the tone one of longing; but the sense is sure.
This sojourn Bonnefoy chooses, within the long path, is reached in
the act of poetry, and is its final and lasting place.

Selected Bibliography

PRIMARY SOURCES

1. Books

Du Mouvement et de l'Immobilité de Douve. Paris: Mercure de France, 1953. *(D)*

Peintures murales de la France gothique. Paris: Paul Hartmann, 1954.

Hier régnant désert. Paris: Mercure de France, 1958. *(HRD)*

L'Improbable. Paris: Mercure de France, 1959. *(I)*

La Seconde simplicité. Paris: Mercure de France, 1961. *(SS)*

Arthur Rimbaud. Paris: Le Seuil, 1961.

L'Anti-Platon. Paris: Galerie Maeght, 1962.

Miró. Milan: Silvana, 1964.

Pierre écrite. Paris: Mercure de France, 1965. *(PE)*

Un rêve fait à Mantoue. Paris: Mercure de France, 1967. *(URM)*

Rome 1630: L'horizon du premier baroque. Paris: Flammarion, 1970. *(B)*

L'Arrière-Pays. Geneva: Skira, 1972. *(AP)*

L'Ordalie. Paris: Galerie Maeght, 1975.

Dans le leurre du seuil. Paris: Mercure de France, 1975. *(DLS)*

Le Nuage rouge. Paris: Mercure de France, 1977. *(NR)*

Rue traversière. Paris: Mercure de France, 1977. *(RT)*

Poèmes. Paris: Mercure de France, 1978. *(P)*

Titres et travaux de Yves Bonnefoy. Paris: n.p., 1980.

Entretiens sur la poésie. Paris: Payot; Neuchâtel: A La Baconnière, 1981. *(E)*

Poèmes. Introduction by Jean Starobinski. Paris: Gallimard, 1982.

2. Prefaces

Preface to *Haiku,* edited by Roger Munier. Paris: Fayard, 1978 *(H)*

Preface to *King Lear,* by Shakespeare. Paris: Gallimard, Collection Folio, 1978.

3. English translations

Of the Movement and the Immobility of Douve. Translated by Galway Kinnell. Athens: University of Ohio Press, 1957.

Written Stone. Translated by Susanna Lang, preface by Sarah Lawall. Amherst: University of Massachusetts Press, 1976.

Complete Poems. Translated by Richard Peaver. New York: Random
House, 1984.

4. Translations by Bonnefoy

a. Shakespeare
Henri IV, part 1, *Jules César, Hamlet, Le Conte d'hiver, Vénus et Adonis.
Le Viol de Lucrèce.* Paris: Club Français du livre, 1957–60.
Jules César. Paris: Mercure de France, 1960.
Hamlet: Suivi d'une Idée de la traduction. Paris: Mercure de France, 1962.
Le Roi Lear. Paris: Mercure de France, 1965.
Roméo et Juliette. Paris: Mercure de France, 1968.
Hamlet et Le Roi Lear. Paris: Gallimard, 1979. Preface by Bonnefoy.
(H)

b. Others
Une chemise de nuit de flanelle, by Leonora Carrington. Paris: Les Pas
perdus, 1951.
"Poèmes de W. B. Yeats." *Argile,* no. 1 (1973), pp. 64–93.

SECONDARY SOURCES

1. Special Journal Issues
L'Arc, no. 66 (October 1976). Articles by, among others, John E.
Jackson, Philippe Jaccottet, Friedhelm Kemp, Roger Munier,
Gaëtan Picon, Jean Starobinski, and Richard Vernier.
World Literature Today, Summer 1979. Edited by Ivar Ivask. Articles by
LeRoy Breunig, Mary Ann Caws, Joseph Frank, Alex Gordon,
Robert Greene, Martin Kanes, Susanna Lang, Sarah Lawall, James
Lawler, Richard Stamelman, Jean Starobinski, and Richard
Vernier.
Sud, 1984. (Colloquium of Cerisy, August 1983.) Articles by, among
others, Mary Ann Caws, Robert Greene, John E. Jackson, John
Naughton, and Richard Stamelman.

2. Articles
Albert, Walter. "Bonnefoy and the Architecture of Poetry." *Modern
Language Notes* 82 (1967): 165–73.
Blanchot, Maurice. "Comment découvrir l'obscur. *NRF* 14
(1959):867–79. ———. "Le Grand refus." *NRF* 14 (1959):678–
89.
Caws, Mary Ann, and **Lawall, Sarah.** "A Style of Silence: Two
Readings of Yves Bonnefoy's Poetry." *Contemporary Literature* 16,
no. 2 (1975):193–217.

Estéban, Claude. "L'Echo d'une demeure." *NRF* 225 (1971):19–34. —
———. "Yves Bonnefoy: L'Immédiat et l'inaccessible." *Critique,* no.
365 (October 1977), pp. 913–48.
Jackson, John E. "L'Espoir d'Yves Bonnefoy." In *Poètes d'Aujourd'hui:
Yves Bonnefoy.* Paris: Seghers, 1976.
Maurin, Mario. "On Bonnefoy's Poetry." *Yale French Studies,* no. 21
(1958), pp. 16–22.
Naughton, John. "*Excarnations:* Yves Bonnefoy's Critique of the Image-
Making Process." *L'Esprit créateur* 22, no. 4 (Winter 1982):37–46.
Prothin, Annie P. "Bibliography of Publications, Studies, and
Translations of Yves Bonnefoy." Ph.D. dissertation, University of
Minnesota.
Vernier, Richard. "Dans la certitude du seuil: Yves Bonnefoy,
aujourd'hui." *Stanford French Review* 2, no. 1 (Spring 1978):139–
47. ———. "From Critical to Poetic Discourse: Bonnefoy and
Poussin." *L'Esprit créateur* 22, no. 4 (Winter 1972):26–36. ———
."Prosodie et silence dans un recueil d'Yves Bonnefoy." *Studia
Neophilologica* 16 (1973):288–97.

3. Chapters in books
Caws, Mary Ann. "Not the Peacock but the Stone." In *The Inner
Theatre of Recent French Poetry: Cendrars, Tzara, Péret, Artaud,
Bonnefoy.* Princeton: Princeton University Press, 1972, pp.141–70.
Jackson, John E. *La Question du moi: T. S. Eliot, Paul Celan, Yves
Bonnefoy.* Neuchâtel: La Baconnière, 1978.
Lawall, Sarah. "Yves Bonnefoy and Denis Roche: Art and the Art of
Poetry." In *About French Poetry from Dada to Tel Quel,* edited by M.
A. Caws. Detroit: Wayne State University Press, 1974, pp. 69–
111.

4. Books
Thélot, Jérôme. *La Poétique d'Yves Bonnefoy.* Geneva: Droz, 1983.
Contains commentaries by Bonnefoy.

Index

DATE DUE

DEMCO 38-297